advantages, problems and solutions of
home-based jobs and businesses

work from home

for a better life and more money

R S Shukla

Excel Books

Copy Editor
Smita Kulshreshth

Art Editor
Abha Bhatia

DTP Designer
Vinod Bhardwaj

Publisher
Anurag Jain

ISBN: 81-7446-307-0

First Edition: New Delhi, 2002

EXCEL BOOKS
A-45, Naraina, Phase I,
New Delhi - 110 028

Published by Anurag Jain for
Excel Books, A-45, Naraina, Phase I,
New Delhi - 110 028 and
printed by him at
Excel Printers, C-206, Naraina, Phase I,
New Delhi - 110 028

CONTENTS

ACKNOWLEDGEMENTS

The author is grateful to a large number of friends, relatives, home-based business owners and working professionals who have contributed with a considerable amount of information and practical advice which has helped immensely in completing this book. Thanks are also due to 'The Times of India', since a few articles, written by the author and published by them, have been reproduced in the book.

chapter 1

opening the door to a better alternative

Improved telephonic communications, liberalising trade with the rest of the globe, advent of Personal Computers, Internet, long hours of commuting, high cost of maintaining a big office and increased socio-economic problems of working away from home are making more and more people inclined to seriously examine the alternative of working from home; some with active encouragement from even the employers. In the West, it is a common phenomena while in India it is gradually becoming a popular alternative.

LAABH HI LAABH

Getting the best out of small business

- **Working from Home:** This option is gradually becoming popular and is attracting young entrepreneurs, retired/retiring people, people who have quit jobs due to long hours of commuting, housewives/ senior citizens who are fit and want to contribute to family income. Many great businesses were born in personal garages, modified verandahs, niches and temporary structures within the house. Suitability of business operations is the prime consideration. Other factors that cannot be ignored are acceptability of the new arrangements by the family, possibility of getting too casual in running the business, setting in of wrong habits like eating or drinking too frequently, lowering of social image, gradually turning into a recluse and ignoring the prime requirement of networking and meeting customers business prospects regularly, etc.

By R S Shukla 'The Times of India', 22 Nov 2001.

NEW OPTIONS

If you have been a sincere 9 to 5 office-goer or work for someone else's business or want to earn something extra as well as be busy at home, the time has come when you should seriously examine the alternative of **working from home,** either on the same job, or a different job, or an additional job or on a business of your own. The same goes for housewives, elderly and retired people, handicapped persons and parents with small children having problems at home.

With the jobs getting more and more scarce, a large number of young and old people are also seeking entrepreneurial ventures to work from home. The list includes senior executives, managers, other salaried staff, children of the entrepreneurs, educated boys and girls, IIT graduates and even fresh MBAs. The twenty-first century offers immense opportunity to do your job or to operate your business from home profitably, comfortably and conveniently.

Mind you, I am saying "from home" and not "at home". The former implies that you have switched the location of your office from a distant place - a place away from your home - to your home. The pattern and quantum of work remains the same. If at all, your output should increase since you have much more time available for work than before. Even if you were spending half an hour one way in commuting to office, saving this time would enable you to have a holiday for a month every year or one extra working month, whatever you wish to choose.

The other and more important implication behind choosing the title is to emphasise that the 'home' is to be used as a "base of operations" and not a "place of all operations". The individuals are expected to move out regularly, seeking business, meeting clients/ customers, networking and checking on the overall business scene.

You are not to become a recluse staying within the confines of the four walls of your home. Instead, you must operate from your home as if it was your company office and venture out as much as required. Operating from home would place a very important resource at your disposal, the "time" saved in daily commuting, which can be utilised to a great business advantage. There are other major benefits as well, but by far, the most important amongst them is the big slice of time saved by giving up the daily office- going routine.

THE BIG TOLL OF COMMUTING

There are commuters in our country who are spending as much time travelling to and fro between their homes and offices as they are spending on their work. Panchwati Express in Maharashtra brings commuters from far-off places to Bombay and hauls them back late in the evening every day. Some of them are spending as much as four and a half hours one way each day. Everyday, thousands of people commute to or from Delhi, Kolkata, Chennai, Mumbai and even lesser important towns (e.g. between Lucknow and Kanpur) by buses and trains, spending scores of hours in the process.

What adds to this tiresome journey is the maddening traffic and debilitating pollution. The stress is taking its toll resulting in lower productivity, increased strife in the family, higher blood pressure, bad hearts, ulcers, chronic headaches, backache, alcoholism, drug addiction etc.

The box below indicates the productive time lost in commuting to the office or workplace. You can judge for yourself the major impact it is making on your total time availability.

Productive Time Lost in Commuting to Office/Workplace Each Year

Up & Down Time in Minutes Per Day	Hours in Each Year (300 Working Days)	Equivalent No. of Lost Per Year
30	150	3.0 Weeks
60	300	6.25 "
90	450	9.5 "
120	600	12.5 "
180	900	19.0 "
360	1800	38.0 "

The huge loss of time as shown above would be acceptable if there were no alternatives available. Indeed, there were no choices available till a few years ago and one had to suffer and endure. Not only the quality and quantity of one's output suffered, or was restricted, but people had to neglect their families also on account of long absences from home.

The nineties have changed it all. The rapid advancement of communication technology has now made it possible for people to communicate to any part of the globe from home. The advent of facsimile machine or fax has made a dramatic impact on communications. Information technology has become a productivity multiplier. Computers can now be operated from homes and laptops.

CHANGES SINCE NINETIES

The major recent changes making it possible and even preferable in many cases to operate efficiently from home are:

1. Availability of better communications to any part of the globe from home or Public Call Offices (PCOs) located nearby.
2. Arrival and acceptance of personal computers, fax machines and Internet.
3. Low initial set-up costs of businesses from home.
4. Fast expanding services sector in India requiring comparatively less office space for business operations. (There are over 5 million retail outlets in India with 96 per cent of these operating in less than 500 sq feet, and the number is likely to more than double in the next few years).
5. More retired people in good health, capable of putting in good work and needing money as well. Likewise, more housewives willing to work from home on account of availability of automated gadgets for kitchen, washing and other household work.

6. Employers encouraging alternatives of working from home, voluntary retirement schemes, golden hand shakes.

7. Enhanced risk-taking ability of the family due to increasing earning potential of wife, husband and other members of the family.

8. Progressive increase in time wasted on commuting to distant offices.

9. Excessive social costs (small children, old parents, other family problems, crime) of being away from home for long hours.

10. Job insecurity due to privatisation, downsizing or closing of establishments/companies, mergers and acquisitions.

One could perceive changes in the pattern of working from the beginning of the nineties. More and more people started to think in terms of quitting their jobs and starting something on their own by operating from their homes. The biggest problem till then was on account of communications. With improved communication and information technology coming in, what would have been a very difficult task otherwise appeared to be within the realm of achievement.

Even many companies realised the advantages of these new factors and some of them started experimenting with the alternative of some of their selected employees being asked to work from home and only periodically report to the corporate office. Many others realised that they could start a small business with much higher returns on account of the changed scenario.

Successful Innovations – Successful People

Veritone India, a Bangalore based computer firm has advised its employees that they need not come everyday to office. The company has provided each of them with a telephone and a personal computer with e-mail at their homes so that they can work from home when needed. The company's offices are open 24 hours a day, seven days a week. Employees are at liberty to come to office at any time of the day or night. All that the company expects is 40 hours work in a week.

With the advancement in micro miniaturisation, the computers of the future will become smaller and smaller. It should not come as a surprise if in a decade the personal computer is accepted as much a part of the home as electrical fitments and telephones. With the advent of e-mail, many new patterns are coming in.

Competitiveness and the corresponding need to cut down costs have induced the top management to have a relook at their office accommodations. Organisations are deciding to retain only that much space which is required for the people whose presence at the office is absolutely essential. The remaining ones are exhorted to go out in the field or work from homes. Even weekly monitoring meetings are held at fixed times in conference rooms at hotels. The so called 'wired executives' are sent out equipped with lap-top computers, e-mail, voice, fax, modems and other communication aids, reporting to their superiors from time to time. Employers welcome it as long as their staff deliver the goods. "Work anywhere, anytime", is the new paradigm.

No wonder, more and more people are opting for working from home. In USA, it was estimated that by the year 2000 AD, 85% of the corporations will be embarking on attractive office strategies, cutting down drastically the core complement at the main office. At the beginning of the twenty-first century, more than 50% of American white collar work-force will be working from home, thanks to the on-going juggernaut of the communication technology.

The Indian scene is equally promising. With the opening up of the economy and liberalisation, many business opportunities are being thrown up. The business in the service sector is bound to go up by leaps and bounds. The technological prop is enabling retired people and housewives to climb up on the bandwagon for part or full time jobs and businesses from home.

NEW PARADIGMS

The mathematics is very simple. In the previous scheme of things, on an average, the husband worked for 8 hours at office and wasted 4 hours every day commuting up and down. The wife looked after the house and the family, not knowing what to do with nearly 4 spare hours, which she could not utilise on anything productive due to the absence of techno-support and scarce opportunities. In the new scheme of things, more than double the number of productive hours are available to the couples when they are working from home. With new opportunities opening up and communications becoming much more convenient, it is possible to conduct full-fledged business operations from home, enabling creative interaction, better team work, efficient marketing and high productivity.

The other big advantage of working from home is that it brings with it an abundant emotional support available from the family. It is true that the proximity also creates some problems which need to be managed. However, being together with the parents, wife, husband, and/ or children is advantageous. More and more people have started production and export businesses, consultancies, property dealership, DTPs, pathological laboratories, business offices, coaching classes, typing schools etc. from their homes with almost everyone in the family chipping in. There are people who are doing it on a part-time basis while others are doing the same as a full-time activity. In fact, many big businesses have started as enterprises from home.

The prime truth is that working from home and operating a worthwhile business or pursuing a worthwhile job or profession is now a feasible, convenient and desirable alternative. It saves you much of daily commuting, which is unproductive, saps your energy and exposes you to pollution hazards. Operating from home also enables you to be close to your family. In other words, you can live a much more balanced life than you had while working at your office, located away from home.

JOBS FROM HOME OR HOME BUSINESS – NOT A BED OF ROSES

A number of issues are to be seriously considered before deciding on this change. A decision to pack up your existing job, shift to home and operate from there will have a deep impact on your on-going work or business. If you quit your job and start a new business from home and do not succeed, discovering too late that you were not cut out for such tasks, you might have lost an opportunity of your lifetime. Remember, it is not a casual few days' shift. This is a permanent change of work style. Once having changed, going back again to the old job may become messier. You might even lose the earlier role or position and others might have happily moved over.

The decision to operate from home is, therefore to be taken after a very careful consideration of the issues involved and after a serious appraisal of yourself. Even after you have succeeded in starting a job or business working from home, serious problems may arise making you much less enthusiastic about the venture than you were at the beginning.

Also, you would be better advised to follow a set of rules, procedures and policies to enable you to settle down in the 'home office' routine. Time and again you will find that the lack of distinctly separated geographical boundaries between the office and home has allowed one disturbing element or the other to creep in and upset the routine. One can correct these provided he or she has the ability to identify them clearly and eliminate them.

If these pitfalls are avoided, there is no reason why you cannot double or triple your income or increase it to still higher limits, along with having the advantage of home and happiness, good health and a busy and satisfied life. Compare it with the job which is always threatened on account of restructuring, mergers, downsizing, voluntary retirement schemes, lock-outs, lay- offs and strikes etc.

NEED FOR PROPER GUIDANCE

By now you must be conscious of the advantages of operating from home. What you will not be aware of are the serious roadblocks, which you can encounter in your venture. Not much guidance is available on how to overcome the problems which one encounters on working from home. Worse, most of you would not even have an idea of the kind of problems you are likely to face. Amongst some, there are exaggerated fears, which later could turn out to be entirely misplaced. Amongst others, there is an undue optimism which is also unwarranted. There is a need for a proper step-by-step guidance for a safe launch and smooth growth.

This book is intended to ensure that if and when you decide to operate from home, you do not fail in your venture. There are physical, psychological, social and other barriers which you must overcome to ensure a successful start. Not only you must go into the venture after a thorough self-analysis, but you have to carry out a regular review and take corrective action also from time to time. The guidelines in the book will ensure that you stay on course and make steady progress - in making money, in leading a stress-free happy life and in enjoying the freedom from the stranglehold of a salaried life in an office located away. For further clarifications and emphasis, a few of my articles, published in the *Times of India* 'Business Opportunities' supplements, have also been given in the book.

The book helps you to decide whether your reasons for starting the business from home are sound and whether you have the necessary entrepreneurial skills and determination to start a business of your own. If yes, then it describes how exactly you should proceed to set up your business at home and grow.

If you follow the proper approach, there is no reason why you should not succeed in reaping the benefits of increased availability of productive time, effective communications and the home environment. The fast pace of modern world has indeed not been kind to our personal lives. The new style can certainly open the door to a better and comfortable way. Some people have rightly described it as the move over from the 'white collar' formal job to an 'open collar', informal but much more productive job.

Finally, even if you are not planning to go into a home business right away, it will be worthwhile going through this book. This will equip you with the correct knowledge, skill and attitude to start a home business even five or ten years later. Your sub-conscious will gradually brace up and make proper preparations to launch you in the new venture when the time for the same arrives.

A Successful Home Business for Suparna Das

Suparna Das, a textile designer specialising in hand painting, worked with a number of firms in Delhi before deciding to quit her job and operate from her home in Dehradun. She gradually set up her office and some production facilities at home engaging a number of operators and embroiders who worked full or part time at Suparna's place. She also developed her own vendors, laying down stiff quality norms, to work in their own respective

Contd...

homes. With the telephone services becoming much more reliable and fast, she was in regular communication with her buyers.

Gradually her business of supplies of saris and fabric to boutiques in Delhi expanded. There were new customers from Bombay as well. To cope up with the increased activities, she hired an accommodation in Delhi which she could use as office-cum-residence during her frequent visits to Delhi. With the expanded set-up, she has been handling business successfully with its Head-quarters at her home in Dehradun. She was also able to carry on despite serious personal problems.

"Working from home was a choice between different alternatives earlier", Suparna explains, "but it has become a necessity, after my mother's death. Now I can look after my father, my home and my business – all from one place with some add-on work from the Delhi Office-cum-residence as well."

chapter 2

self analysis: can you work from home?

Working from home is a major decision and has to be taken after a thorough understanding of the major problems involved, by analysing yourself, identifying areas where you should develop yourself and making a time-bound plan to improve yourself. Give this aspect the importance it deserves.

You may not realise, but working under the same roof where your family lives is not easy. You may not be able to create the kind of professional environment which is needed by you. Your spouse, children or other members of the family might not appreciate the idea at all and might like to be around you in what they think is their idea of being a help. In actual fact, these little incidents do not allow you to settle and concentrate.

When **Colonel Bery** retired from Army, he wanted to write articles and books on defence matters. He, however, found that he could not get the long stretches of free time which he needed for this venture. His wife would come with a cup of tea and some snacks every once in a while and start discussing gossip and domestic problems. By the afternoon the children would be back from college/institute with their latest share of gossip to exchange. Colonel Bery very soon switched over from writing to playing golf.

Anita Malik, was however, much more firm and astute, when she started her beauty parlour from one of the rooms of her home. She also had her share of disturbances. Her in-laws were also staying with her. After a few days of debating and vacillation, she told her family members of her requirements to be alone, time-wise and work-place wise, when her parlour was open. She herself ensured that even if there were no customers, she remained in the parlour keeping herself busy with other chores like maintenance, cleaning, reading etc. Gradually, the family got adapted to the new routine. Her clientele grew so much that after a few months she had to relocate her parlour in the rented premises next door.

MAJOR PROBLEMS IN WORKING FROM HOME

Having settled on the point that working from home could be a profitable proposition, let us examine the major problems from this mode of operation. These are:

- **Rushing** into a home-based venture **without analysing** if you are cut out for it.
- A **faulty selection** of the job/ job pattern or a home-based business.
- **Not having adequate space, furniture, equipment and supplies for the home office.** Lack of imagination/ innovation in establishing the office and managing from it.
- **Interruptions** from family, children, relatives and friends: When you are present in the house, problems, big or small, need your attention as a matter of habit. Unless you make it a point to treat your "office at home" as "office away from home", you will find yourself being subjected to a continuous stream of distractions.
- **Irregular Routine**: This happens on account of change of working pattern. Naturally a close examination of your routine and sub-routines will be necessary to ensure that undesirable practices do not creep in.
- **Feeling of Isolation**: The psychological strokes and satisfaction one gets from colleagues and the office environment will be absent and can be missed very badly by some.

- **Lack of Privacy**: People, relatives, friends, neighbours keep dropping in. At least, some of them keep doing so out of curiosity to find how well you are doing. This unwanted intrusion is likely to result in fouling up your mood.
- **Fall in esteem value**: You will suddenly find that the response and respect you got from your relatives, friends and neighbours when you had the job, gets diluted when you start operating from home. People do not take you seriously till such time as you make a substantial progress in the venture. At least, some of them hold the view that you were misled in leaving the job and trying to make a second career.

It is necessary that all the above problems are countered efficiently through a combination of measures. These are as follows:

- A proper self-analysis involving a deep examination of yourself to find if you are mentally and psychologically equipped to operate from home and do well.
- A proper examination of the job or job-mix or a home business you wish to undertake from home. In case of the latter, a proper selection of the product or service.
- Have a separate space earmarked for the office at home. This requires imagination and innovation.

- Learn how to manage from this office including discharging basic marketing, financial and accounting functions.
- Treat yourself to be away from home when dealing with the problems/interruptions at home during your working hours.
- Establish a proper office routine. It is not necessary that the availability of extra time at home should keep you busy throughout the day. You must have time for the family, rest and recreations. These are necessary and will contribute to your personal efficiency in the business.
- Obtain a separate telephone, or at least a separate extension.
- Ensure that your printed materials i.e. letter heads, stationery and business cards etc. indicate that you are a serious professional. Communication via telephone should be business-like and pleasant. Do not allow children to talk on your business line.
- Establish self-management and business management goals on daily, weekly, monthly and even longer periods. Develop an attitude that you 'work' from home. At home do not allow paper work, books, files, office equipments clutter the rooms beyond a point where it hurts home comforts. If need be, you may take advice from consultants or colleagues on space saving storage system.

- Be positive and enthusiastic in your venture and obtain help and cooperation from your family, customers and friends. If you are employed, obtain the requisite support from your colleagues as well as your seniors.
- Be aware of wrong habits setting in and get rid of them.

The above-mentioned points and a few others have been incorporated in the box below to serve as your permanent guide.

Ten Commandments for Smooth Working from Home	
1.	Analyse yourself thoroughly to ascertain if you are suited for the home-based job/business. Choose the job/job pattern or business with care.
2.	Have a separate room or physically partitioned space for your office. If necessary, optimise, innovate and create more space. Keep getting rid of the litter regularly.
3.	Establish an office and a proper work schedule and stick to it. Have a schedule for rest and recreation also. Dress for success. Set goals every day, week, month, quarter, half year and year (choose appropriate intervals), apart from daily goals, which are a must.
4.	Observe time management. Look out periodically for time-stealers, which have a tendency to creep in. Economise/control time spent on telephones, conferences, visitors and interruptions. Control TV time and do something additional while watching the idiot-box. Do best activities at best times of your body cycle.
5.	Work 'from home' and not 'at home'. Make at least one business trip every day. Your home should be a base, not a fenced prison house.
6.	Your letter heads, visiting cards, stationery should indicate you are a serious professional. The same should apply to your business calls. As far as possible have a separate phone or business line. Have printed cheques, if possible.

Contd....

7. Anticipate personal/psychological/behavioural problems between you and your spouse/ children/family due to your working from home and devise solutions to ensure love, affection and support from them. Cultivate neighbours.
8. Develop and maintain proper information linkages. Don't over-socialise. Also don't over-commute. Instead, communicate.
9. Develop customer orientation. Make and maintain customers. Follow realistic marketing.
10. Manage finances properly. Ensure regular cash generation. Provide for emergency money.

KEY QUESTIONS FOR SELF ANALYSIS

Analysing yourself is an extremely important step. It is necessary to know whether you are cut out for a home-based venture. You must seriously look before you leap.. Begin by asking questions given at the box below.

Are you Ready to Work from Home - Key Questions

- Will you like a home routine? Sometimes, it might involve sustained hard work all by yourself. Is your home environment conducive to working from home?
- Do you have the experience, aptitude and key entrepreneurial qualities (listed in next para) to take on the challenges? If not, can you acquire/ develop these attributes through work, self development and learning?
- For starting a business from home, do you have enough information? If not, can you develop information linkages to get the vital inputs on your product or service, prices, promotion, distribution, finances, competition, industrial relations, technology and important environmental factors?
- Do you have a product or service you can produce/ supply/ market readily or after a reasonable period which is likely to

Contd....

give you profit for a few years i.e., till you switch over to the next one?

- Do you have your target market and answers to key marketing questions such as who, what, where, when and how to sell?
- What form of ownership you would prefer – proprietorship or partnership? In case of the latter, do you have an adaptable nature?
- Do you have enough capital and reserves? Can you arrange the same?
- **Will you survive if the business fails?**

Key Entrepreneurial Qualities

The entrepreneurial qualities, which a person aspiring to work from home should possess or should strive to possess, are as follows:

- Problem-solving – An attitude to welcome, expect and solve problems.
- Setting personal targets.
- Creativity, innovation and initiative.
- Persistence, drive, energy and determination.
- Firm faith in planning/follow-up cycle.
- Communication and persuasive ability.
- Human relations ability.
- Technical knowledge and basics of marketing and financial functions.

- Moderate risk-taking, while keeping firm control of your money.
- Self-discipline, self-confidence & commitment.

It is said that entrepreneurial qualities cannot be taught, but they can be acquired. If you go through the above list and find that you do not have some of the qualities, make a step-by-step plan to acquire/develop the same. As you will notice, they are not extraordinary attributes and a normal person should have them or develop them through constant practice, trial and error. Since you will be operating on your own, it is desirable that you are at least aware of these so that the same can be developed by you, should you find that you lack some of them to some extent. If you wish, you can also undergo a short course at an entrepreneurial institute. A good book on entrepreneurship will also be of help.

Basic Steps

Once you have analysed yourself and found that you are ready to start your job from home or a home business venture, the next steps to be taken by you are as follows:

1. Select the intended job/job-mix or product for the intended business service.
2. Develop your business plan if you are going in for a small business.
3. Survey/locate/create/set-up/manage office, develop business identity, start/complete essential formalities and establish/ follow a work schedule.

4. Create proper financial structure, bank account, credits, insurances etc. Do basic marketing and financial functions.
5. Review performance from time to time.
6. Maintain harmonious domestic relationships. Prevent wrong habits from creeping in.
7. Earn more and enjoy more.

In the next two chapters, we shall discuss the subject of selection of a job or business suitable for conducting from home.

Profile of a Professional Working from Home

After 32 years of working on different assignments, the author left a good job with an industry at Kandla Free Trade Zone and returned to his home in NOIDA in 1990. Since then, operating from home, he has been able to:

Establish and run a Management Consultancy. Author 12 books including the current one. Contribute 35 articles for the Time of India Lecture at Institutes/Organisations regularly. Function as a Vice President/President of Noida Management Association for 4 years.

Attend to a no. of major family commitments. Help his son for preparation/selection in a prestigious organisation.

Rebuild his health lost due to rigours of work in the jobs.

Been to a minimum of two holidays every year fulfilling a life long dream of seeing his beautiful country.

OOO

chapter 3

selecting a home-based job

If you are wanting to do a home-based part or full-time job and have a problem of choosing the best option, guidelines given in this chapter will help.

SELECTING A JOB

If you are looking forward to take on a job to be performed from home, short-list your options with the following guidelines for the jobs which can conveniently be performed from home:

1. Those which require less interruptions and more concentration.
2. Where tasks/targets to achieve are clear and clearly specifiable and performance is easily measurable.
3. Good understanding with clients/ customers/ employers as applicable.
4. Less material/ resources required to be brought and stored at home.
5. Where the alternative job requires too much commuting.
6. Lesser face-to-face contact.
7. Where performance review can be done once a week or fortnight i.e. longer than what you normally would do at the office with your superior/employer.

If you have more than one shortlisted option, select the best option considering the following:

- Your expertise and attraction for the work.
- The financial returns
- Potential for growth

- Potential for more lucrative options in future e.g. job mixes, job-business mix or eventually graduating into a full-fledged business.

JOB MIXES

You could take on a mix of job and a business, with the intention to gradually venture into a full-fledged business of your own. A large number of employed persons are already doing it.

For example, you could perform extra work relating to purchasing, personnel, recruiting, programming etc. i.e., the job you were doing in your old organisation on agreed rates and terms. Alternatively, the organisation might ask you to work from home on the job you were doing at office and report on agreed schedules.

The above modes of work can be combined to give the following job patterns at home till you are ready to start your full-fledged business from home:

- **'Job plus' pattern:** Working on something extra at home while retaining the job. It is felt that a minimum of 10-12 hours should be spent per week on work at home to make the effort worthwhile.
- **'Part-time' plus pattern:** Having a part time job and combining it with another part-time job or additional hours of work from home.
- **'Spin-off' pattern:** Taking on additional work from the previous employer and doing it at home. Also, starting a business serving the clients of your old organisations.

- **'Pocket money' pattern:** Taking on a light work at home to earn enough to provide for your pocket money. Students taking this on would have an added advantage of some job exposure.
- **'One plus one' pattern:** One working spouse is on a full-time job while the other is pursuing a business at home and is also looking after children and/or parents. This pattern has been followed by even a number of husbands where the wife is employed in a better job.
- **'Production mix' pattern:** Depending upon the product, space requirement and administrative constraints, a small scale industry, an ancillary industry, a tiny enterprise or a small scale (industry related) service and business related enterprise can be started with the office at home and the production undertaken either at home or at a place away from home. More information on these can be obtained from the District industries officer or any officer connected with Small Scale Industry (SSI) sector.

JOBS WHICH CAN BE DONE FROM HOME

Some of the jobs which can be done from home are given below:

Accountancy	Insurance Agent
Advertising Copywriter	Insurance Survey or Inspection
Advertising Sales Representative	Interpreter
Administration	Interviewer
Advocate (Lawyer)	Inventory Executive

Contd...

- Airline Ticketing
- Architect
- Audit
- Book Keeper
- Booking Agent
- Book Keeping
- Buying Agent
- Claim Processor
- Computer Supply
- Computer Programmes
- Computer System Analyst
- Computer Technicians
- Cost Analyst
- Consultant Correspondent
- Desktop Publishing
- Editing
- Event Management
- Financial Functions
- Graphic Designer
- Headhunter
- Market Planning
- Market Research
- Market Survey
- Management Accounting
- Medical Advice
- News Reading
- News Reporting
- Passports
- Personnel Search
- Personnel Recruitment
- Private Detective
- Public Relations Specialist
- Project Reports
- Purchasing Representatives
- Property Dealer
- Research
- Reservations
- Sales Executive
- Secretary
- Social Researcher
- Software Engineer
- Surveyor
- Stenographer
- Shares, Stocks, Investments
- Translator
- Tourist Guide
- Travel Agent
- Type Setting
- Word Processor

A Job After His Heart

FLT. LT A B Sigamony (Retd) settled down in his newly allotted flat in JalavayuVihar, NOIDA on retiring from IAF after his full service. A few months after shifting to NOIDA, he joined a private company as its Chief Executive. Although he liked the new organisation and the job, he was not comfortable with the long hours he had to spend in the company as well as the long distance he had to commute up and down from NOIDA.

After serving for a couple of years, Sigamony found the opening he was seeking. He accepted the job of Executive Secretary of NOIDA Management Association which had a large membership of managers from Industry, business and government organisations. However, the Association, affiliated to All India Management Association, was a young organisation and did not have its own premises and required the Executive Secretary to operate from his home.

Sigamony more than welcomed the offer, created an office at his home and was operational within a very short time. He would venture out every day meeting prospective members as well as the existing ones, arranging major and minor events of the association including management seminars, workshops, lectures and even large conventions in addition to discharging his other executive functions relating to the office, liaison, purchasing etc. He was happy and comfortable with the job till he left it after a few years on account of new and pressing family requirements.

"Working from home was the best thing that happened to me", Sigamony explained, "I found a job of my liking, eliminating the non-productive long hours of commuting for the previous job. Despite the demands of a challenging assignment, I always found sufficient time for my family."

ooo

chapter 4

choosing your home-based business

While a 'job' being done from home is easy to be replaced by another one, the same cannot be said of a home-based business. The home-based business should therefore be selected with much more care after checking all relevant factors.

KEY QUESTIONS

For taking up a business from home, you must respond positively to the following questions while identifying the options:

- Will you enjoy that specific business activity and multi-level responsibilities?
- Will you enjoy spending time in your house on business work?
- Are you aware of the essential technical, marketing and financial details of the product or service you wish to deliver from home? If not, then do you have someone who is competent to perform these functions on your behalf? Is the business allowed to be run from home?
- Do you like your neighbourhood and do you get along with neighbours?
- Are you having adequate space readily available or easily available after structural modifications in the house? Is the business allowed to be run from home?
- What is the proximity to the suppliers of your materials as well as of your business market?
- Can you counter negative emotions from wife/children and very close relatives.

While making a decision, do remember that many Indian and international giants have started their business from home. Companies like **Ford Motors, Walt Disney, Reader's Digest,**

Play-boy Magazine, Hewlett Packard, Gillette Razor, Apple Computers are some of the global giants which started this way. In India firms like Telemecanique and Controls and Stencil Apparels, also had their origins at homes. The important thing to remember is that this is something you should enjoy and have a capacity of doing it in an excellent way. Do identify your best hobbies/interests, talents or expertise, which could be transformed into a business.

Selecting the Basic Business Line

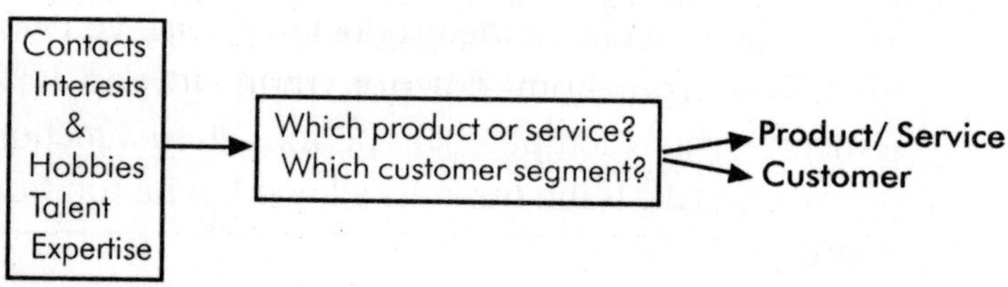

For example, you could consider doing the following if you have aptitude for:

- Selling old collections.
- Creative arts and crafts.
- Organising travel, adventure sports.
- Direct selling, selling cosmetics.
- Taking dance or exercise classes.
- Running a recording studio.
- Offering lessons in sports.

- Running a coaching institute.
- Doing interior designing/decorations.
- Event-Management.

Meet Dadi Balsara, The Billionaire NRI at Singapore
Starting as a 22 year-old LIC agent, earning Rs 600 a month, Dadi Balsara was soon looking for a change because he felt he could do much better utilising his extraordinary energy and personal talents. A palmist, pedologist, psychologist, face-cum-foot reader and a fourth dan black belt in Karate, Dadi left the job and started a consultancy from home. Soon he became very influential and popular advising even Presidents and Prime Ministers. His ambitions took him to Singapore where he is an NRI making perfumes in Singapore, ceramics in Malaysia, jeans in Korea, watches in Switzerland and natural mineral water in India with his assets running into billions of dollars. Working from home was the ideal launching pad for him.

THE BIG QUESTION

How does one identify what he or she likes best? These activities are the ones, which evoke the positive response to following questions/suggestions.

- You like doing them the most.
- You get so involved doing them that you lose track of time.
- You feel most energised while doing these activities.
- You like to discuss them and speak with authority on such subjects.

- The memories, mementos and photographs relating to the activities are valued by you most.
- Important items in newspapers or magazines related to these activities are read by you with interest.

A few more suggestions to identify activities you like best are listed in the following para. The later paras suggest the way to identify the basic business line or product or service you might wish to pursue as a follow-up of the identified preferred activity.

Identifying Things You Enjoy Most

1. What do you read first in newspapers/magazines?
2. What interests you so much that you lose track of time?
3. What are you doing when you feel most alive and energised?
4. What do you take prompt action on? What do you delay?
5. What mementos and photographs do you cherish most? What do you collect?

Having Identified Your Prime Interests, Identify the Basic Business Idea by Asking Following Questions

1. Can you sell what your prime interests are, in the form of a product or service?
2. What marketing segment can you target?

3. If there is a demand and will it sustain itself? Who are the competitors? Are there any new competing products?

4. What innovations are possible, which will please customers the most?

5. What is the likely price, business volumes and break-even points ? What are the financial requirements to set up, start and run the business and do you have them or can you arrange them?

6. When and where should you start?

7. How will you start ? What is the business plan?

BUSINESS FROM A HOBBY OR INTEREST

You could, for example:

1. Become a travel guide, an airline staff or a travel agency worker.

2. Become an interior decorator.

3. Offer tennis/badminton/cricket/karate lessons.

4. Become a dog trainer.

5. Give lessons on singing/dancing/speaking languages.

6. Sell antiques.

7. Buy/Sell/Rent cars, two wheelers or property.

8. Run cookery class.
9. Plan parties, birthdays, weddings and other events.
10. Lecture, be a tutor, hold seminars/workshops in your area of expertise.

BUSINESS INVOLVING YOUR TIME/EXPERTISE

You could also increase your options by choosing a business which others do not have time or expertise to do. For example, you could:

1. Provide a helpline for odd jobs.
2. Offer painting, whitewashing, window washing, special cleaning, fan wiping, car washing, home maintenance, repair services of electrical appliances.
3. Do estate planning/management.
4. Do investment counselling, income tax/sales tax consultant.
5. Do income tax service, payment of telephone/ electricity/club bills.
6. Do inventory management.
7. Offer pick-up and delivery service.
8. Operate a security service, detective service, special home security service.
9. Organise gardening/carpentry/bathroom fixtures, plumbing, plant care, provide plants for parties.
10. Run a mobile computer repair service.

There are many other businesses which could be started by putting things you have in or around the house to work. You could use your kitchen for special catering services or catering classes, use an extra room as day-care centre or for taking classes in your area of specialisation. Similarly, you could use your vehicle for different services to customers e.g. Mobile lunch service.

More than 450 small businesses have been listed at the end of this chapter at Appendix. You can carefully go through this list to check if some of these find your fancy.

Having selected your first few choices, you have to relate them to the market and funds availability to choose the most preferred line. A product or service so selected must be needed by the market during the next 5 years or so. A lesser period can only be accepted if the profit margin is higher.

Having chosen your preferred business, you have to decide on appropriate pattern of working from an office located at home and create this office if it is not readily available. What pattern of working will suit you best? Where would be your office located, in or around your home? It could even be in the basement or on the rooftop. It could be part of your porch, garage or a niche in the sloping roof. We shall discuss the patterns of working and office-creation in the chapters to follow.

However, at this stage, it is essential that you write down your plan of action, your 'business plan'. A written business plan will clarify many doubts and will focus on where you are now and where you want to be at a specified time. This is not just a paper exercise. Many entrepreneurs have attributed their success to a properly written business plan covering all activities.

THE BUSINESS PLAN

The important components of a business plan are as follows:

- Self assessment of strengths and weakness.
- Form of desired ownership: sole proprietorship, partnership, company franchising.
- Business plan: buying an existing business or starting a new business.
- Sources of funds: equity or debt- capital.
- Facilities plan: location analysis, physical facilities requirements.
- Management plan: strategy, objectives, human resource management, motivation, communication, computerisation, security, risk management etc.
- Financial plan: record keeping, cash control, accounting statements, budgets.
- Operational control plan: production, purchasing, inventory control.
- Marketing Plan: strategy, market segments, market-mix, market research, pricing, consumer behaviour, personal selling, promotion strategy.

- Legal/statutory requirements.
- Follow-up/review cycle.

Check all Important Points in Advance

Shifting to his newly rented bigger residence, VK Malhotra was happy on two counts. First, his children got a bigger room they had been clamouring for. Second, he could also operate his courier agency from the new residence.

His euphoria, however, was short-lived since his landlord objected to running the agency from the residence as this was not the part of the lease agreement. Within a month, Malhotra had to shift his agency to a nearby commercial complex. 'I wish', Malhotra confessed, 'I had done my planning properly and had cleared this point with the landlord before signing the agreements'. A properly thought-out researched and written business-plan would have been the ideal starting point'.

Important points, during implementation, and even during the preparation/ writing of a business plan are as follows:

- Stress on objectives and how they are to be achieved with milestones.
- Make it a working, non-bulky document. If needed, have half page action summaries for each function.
- Strike a proper balance between all functions.
- Plan for contingencies - both positive and negative.
- Include a monthly/ fortnightly review.
- Update the plan every six months or at any other suitable interval.

- Plan should be specific and for a foreseeable period.

In this and the previous chapter, we have discussed how to select a job or a job-mix or a job-business mix or a pure business to be performed by you from home. Let us then proceed further to examine as to how does one establish a 'Home-office at home'.

Where a Business – Plan would have Gertainly Helped

An entrepreneur, with nearly five years' experience of manufacturing HB pencils, decided to start his own unit in the backyard of his house and operate from home. Instead of acquiring planning plant and machinery he decided to fabricate them on his own. This resulted in inordinate delays, gradual depletion of working capital and mounting liabilities. With a weakened financial base, he had additional setbacks. While sales tax on pencils in the neighbouring states was exempted, it wasn't so in his own. Besides, there was a problem in getting bulk raw material (wood) since his state followed a strict policy for forest protection. To top it up, the richer and larger manufacturers were offering credit terms which were much superior to his own.

Gradually his unit started losing its financial health and was eventually declared sick.

"I wish I had written a proper business-plan," he confessed later, "I would then have been guided more by logic than my emotions and avoided an irretrievable disaster."

Appendix

Businesses which can be run/organised from home are:

Accounting

Aquarium Maintenance

Aquarium Supplier

Action Serving

Adventure Sports

Advertising/ Copywriting

Aerobic classes

After - hours work

Airline Ticketing

Alarm & Security Services

Animal show organising/ judging

Answering Service

Antique Selling/Location/Repair/ Restoration

Apparels/ Garments Retailing

Appliances - Repair/Refinishing

Appraising - Precious Metals
- Personal Collections

Architecture

Arts - Instructions, Studio, Repairs

Astrology

Athletic Equipment Repair

Auctioning

Audit

Auto Dealership/ Services/ Brokering

Auto Licensing

Ayurved

Baby Sitting

Beauty Parlour

Bed and Breakfast Service

Billing and Invoicing Service

Bonsai

Book Binding

Book Keeping

Booking/ Travel Agent

Bouquest Delivery Service

Boutiques

Bridal Make-up

Bronze Work

Building Inspection Service

Building Restoration/Preservation

Bus Services

Business Broker

Business Cards

Business Consultant

Cabinet Making

Cake Decoration

Caning Repair

Canning fruits, Juices & Preservatives

Car Repairs

Car Sales - Second Hand

Car Washing & Polishing

Career Institutes

Carpentry

Carpet Cleaning

Carpet Restoration

Catering

Catering Services

Ceiling Fan Cleaning

Ceiling Repair

Chat Shop

Chess Instructions

Chess/ Carom Club

Child Care Services

Cleaning Services

Clearing/Shifting Services

Clothing Alterations

Clowns for Parties

Clubs

Communications - Telephone, STD, ISD, Fax

Composing on PC

Computer Classes for Children

Computer Programming

Computer Systems Analysts

Computer-Repair/Maintenance

Construction

Consultancies

Contest Organiser

Conveyances (Taxis, Buses, Pick-ups)

Cooking Classes

Cooking Instructor

Copying Services (Audio-tapes, Computer discs, Photocopier, Videotapes)

Copywriter

Costtime Renting

Counselling

Courier Services

Crafts Business

Creches

Cricket Coach

Cyber Cafes

Dance Therapy

Dancing Instructions

Data - Converting Service

Data - Processing Service

Data Base Administrator

Data Entry Clerk

Day-care - Adults/Children

Debugging Software

Delivery Services - Flowers/ Parcels

Desk Top Publisher

Diet Counsellor

Direct Mail Advertising

Disk Formatting Service
Disk Jockey Service
Dog Trainer
Dog Walker/ Exerciser
Domestic Services
Dry Cleaning
Dyeing
Economic Adviser
Editing
Education
Educational Support
Eldercare
Electrical Jobs
E-mail
Embroidery
Employment Agency
Energy Consultation
Engraving
Entertaining
Environment Safety
Errand Service
Escort Service
Etiquette Training
Event Management
Executive Search
Exercise Instructions
Exhibition Gallery
Exporter
Eyesight Trainer
Fashion Designing
Fashion Wear
Fast Foods
Film Processing
Financial Services/ Adviser
Fire Consultancy
First Aid Training
Fitness School
Flour Mill
Flower Shop/ Arrangements
Food Delivery
Foreign Exchange Advice
Freelance Writer
Freight Broker
Fund Raising
Furniture Delivery/Maintenance/ Supply/Hire
Games Counsellor
Garden Designer/Cave
Gems and Jewellery
General Merchants
Gift Baskets/Buying/ Wrapping
Gift Shops
Glass Etching/Repair
Gold Smith
Golf Instructions
Graphic Designer

Greeting Card Designer/Artist
Gunsmith
Hair Dressing
Handicraft Making
Handwriting Analyst
Handyman
Hauling Service
Health Clinics
Herb Farm
Hiring Cars
Holiday Lighting & Decoration
Holiday Planning
Home Care Agencies
Home Furnishings
Home Tuitions
Homeopathy
Horseback Riding Service
Hospitals
Hotels
House Painter
House Security Consultant
House Sitter
Housing
Ice Cream Parlour
Image Consultant
Importer
Income Tax Consultancy
Insurance
Insurance Agent
Interior Decorator
Interior Design
Internet Training, E-mail Publishing, Web Site designing & Marketing Consultant
Interpreter
Interviewer
Inventory Controller
Investment
Investment Counselling
Job Placements
Journalist
Kids Taxi Service
Kirtan Mandali Arranging
Kitty Parties ArrangIng
Knitting Garments, Hand or Machine
Landscaping/ Care Service
Language Teaching.
Laundry Service
Lawn Care
Lawyer Consultancy
Leasing
Library
Loan Broker
Locksmith
Lost Pet Location

Loud Speakers Hiring
Maid Service
Mailing List Agency
Management Accounting
Management Consultancy
Management Training
Manicurist
Manufactures' Representative
Manuscript Editing
Market Planning
Market Research
Marketing Consultant
Marriage Arrangements
Marriage Cosultancy
Marriage Counselling
Massage Service
Mediator
Medical Clinic/Medical Technician
Medical Transcription
Medicare
Medicines
Mehandi (Henna) Classes
Mini Golf Course
Mobile Auto Care
Mobile Disc Jockey
Mobile Hair Dresser
Motels
Music Classes
Networking Classes
Networking Organisation
News Reporter
Newsletter Publisher
Niche Greeting Cards
Notary Service
Numerology
Nursery-Rave Plants
Nurses Agency
Nursing Homes
Office Automation
Operation Research
Out-of-town Business Service
Packing/ Unpacking Service
Paging Services
Painting Training
Palmistry
Pandits - Arranging
Parent Education
Parental Counselling
Parties Arranging
Patent Searcher
Pathology Laboratories
Pay Roll Services
Paying Guests
Payroll Preparation Service
PCO Operator/ Ownership

Personal Care
Personal Chef
Personal collections
Personal Organiser
Personnel Consultant
Pest Control
Pest Control Service
Pets
Pets & Related Services, Pet care
Photography
Photostat
Piano Time
Picnics - Arranging
Picture Frames
Picture Framing
Placement Services
Placements
Plumbing
Potter
Pre and Post Natal Counselling
Presentation Service
Printing
Printing Letter Heads, Visiting Cards etc.
Private Investigator
Project Report Controller
Proof Reader
Proof Reading Service
Property Renting/ Selling/ Buying
Providing Assorted Services
Providing Passports
Provision Shop
Public Opinion Analysis Survey
Public Relations, Professionals
Publicity Service
Publishing Local Directories
Purchasing Agent Service
Purchasing Properties
Reading Service
Receptionist
Recording Studio
Referral Services
Refreshing & Restoring
Rental Service
Renting Autos
Renting Land
Renting Managers & Supervisors
Repair Service
Repairs
Research and Analysis
Resources
Restaurant
Restoration Consultant
Resume Writing
Retailing
Retirement Counselling

Retirement Counselling Researcher
Reunion Planning
Reunion Organiser
Sales Representatives
Sales Tax Counselling
Seamstress/ Tailors
Secretary
Security Counselling
Security Services
Self - Publisher
Seminar/ Workshop Promoter
Sewer Cleaning
Share Broking
Shares, Securities, Mutual Funds
Shifting Houses
Sighseeing Guide Service
Skeet Wending
Skin Care Products
Snacks Shop
Social Worker
Sofa repair
Sofa Repairing
Software Engineer
South Indian Foods
Speciality Photographer
Speciality Travel & Tours
Speechwriter
Spices - Home Supplies
Sport Event Management
Sports Coaching
Sports Photography
Stationary Shop
Steno Services
Stenographer
Stitching
Stock Broker
Storage
Studio
Surveyor
Sweet Shops
Sweets
Systems Analysts
Tailoring
Tax Consultancy
Taxi Services
Teaching
Telemarketing
Tennis Coach
Tent House
Textile Designing
Tiffin Supplies
Time Saving Devices
Tourism
Translation
Transportation, Pick-up Vans

- Travel Agency
- Tree Trimmer
- Tuitions
- Type Setting
- Typing
- Typist Training
- Upholstery Repairs/Cleaning/ Changing
- Urban Planner
- Vaastu Consultant
- Valet Parking
- Video Games
- Video Photography
- Waiters Providing
- Wake-up calls
- Ware Housing
- Watch Repair
- Weight-loss Counselling
- Wellness Instructor
- White Washing
- Window Cleaning
- Word Processor
- Yoga Coaching at Home
- Zipper Repairs

LAABH HI LAABH

Small Business: Source of wealth for many, stepping stone to big business for some

- Small business is not only an inextricable part of any society, but has also been a stepping stone to big business, and a source of wealth and employment Late Gulshan Kumar's Super Cassette Industries, Flex Industries and Hindustan Computer Limited (HCL) are large businesses that have grown from humble origins, Ford Motor Co., Hewlett-Packard, Amway Nike, Gillette, Reader's Digest and Walt Disney are similar success stories from abroad. The ubiquitous presence of the small businesses should be evident from the scores of PCOs, courier agencies, day care centres, astrologists, event managers, grocery stores, website designers, etc. that continue to come up in the neighbourhood at regular intervals. With the service sector poised for huge growth in the next few years due to improved communications, Internet and liberalisation, small business is also ready to expand exponentially. This is a tremendous business opportunity for entrepreneurs, retired/retiring/ VRS people, housewives, elderly but fit people, as well as jobholders with surplus time. However, as one embarks on a small business, the following important points ought to be kept in mind.
- **Are you Temperamentally Suited for Business?** Business is not a casual, short time affair but a sustained long-term involvement. For some it could be a seven days a week, 24 hours a

day involvement. It calls for calculated risk taking as opposed to rash gambles, a cool head, considerable self-discipline and a capacity to develop inter-personal relationships. Just as not everyone can become a successful cricketer, footballer or fashion designer, similarly not everyone can do well in business, Hence, look elsewhere if you are not made for business.

- **Careful Selection of Product/ Service:** Your familiarity with the product/service you wish to launch is important, but it is more important to determine whether a market exists, and will continue to exist, for a long time for this product/service. Many people have ignored the latter aspect and have launched businesses only because they were confident of their knowledge of the product, and assumed that it would sell. Very soon they found out that the product had not takers. While you should select the product/service applying the CITE (contacts, interest, talent and experience) principle, the business must be launched after a thorough market survey, formal or informal. Simultaneously, examine the market environment, present and future, trends, competition, new products and technologies, availability of raw materials, consumer behaviour as well as regulatory environment, which includes restrictions, taxes, aids, incentives, subsidies, etc. Remember, being in the right business is as important as managing the business rightly. Ensure that subordinates are not kept tied down inordinately affecting their performance. Appreciate the value of your time as well as that of others.

LAABH HI LAABH

Making a Small Business a Success

- **Financial Matters:** This is as important as product selection and marketing issues. Carefully work out the real costs of starting the business, running it, your own expense requirements and your financial goals. Also work out your sources of funds and their availability. It is suggested that this could be done monthly for your first year of business, and quarterly for the next few years. It is always better to underestimate your revenues and overestimate your expenditures. Remember, subsidies/aids from the government always get delayed. Hence, do not link their availability to fixed-time critical requirements. Similarly, there will always de delays in receiving money from accounts receivables, so do not bank exclusively, or even too much on this source. One of the early decisions you will have to take is whether to buy an existing business or to start a new one from scratch. People well versed with financial function are advised to work out a Profit & Loss Statement and a Balance Sheet for each year. Establish break-even points and if possible, undertake a return-on-investment analysis.

- **Obtain Practical Business Experience:** Ideally, if you have some practical experience in trading of the proposed product or service, you are best equipped to launch your own business. If you are not that fortunate, then try and acquire practical experience in any practical activity related to your product, or a family of similar products.

  Collect as much data, information and facts as possible in the pre-launch phase. At the risk of repetition, it is emphasised that practical business experience with an ongoing establishment is an extremely valuable asset to have before launching one's own business.

- **Organisation and Staffing:** The most preferred type of organisation for the small business is sole proprietorship. The other alternatives are a partnership concern, a limited company and franchising. All of them have their pluses and minuses. In a partnership concern, it is necessary that you have the confidence of getting along with your partner. If your business involves frequent absences from the establishment, it would be desirable to have a close relative, e.g., father, wife, brother or sister assisting in your business. Alternatively, a trustworthy friend or a professional will do. Initially, start with minimum staff but do keep some others in mind whom you can recruit when the workload goes up, or when the existing staff switches over to another employer.

- **Location of Premises:** A decision on location of premises should be taken after all relevant factors have been taken into account. These include acquisition cost or rent, renovations required, suitability for business operations, security, regulatory requirements, transportation facilities, availability of raw material/goods, accessibility to market, maintenance facilities, attitude of neighbours or the landlord, distance from your residence, disposal of effluents, anti-pollution requirements, etc.

* By R S Shukla 'The Times of India' Dt. 8 and 15 March 2001.

OOO

chapter 5

creating the home office - comfortable, convenient, functional and professional

Once you have taken a decision to do a job or business from home, the next step is to create an appropriate office which should not only help you to function efficiently but convey the correct impression to your business customers/visitors also.

THE NEED FOR INGENUITY

If you are lucky, you might have a separate room already at home which can conveniently be converted into an office. This is however, not generally the case. It will need considerable ingenuity from you to carve out your office within your home. You will have to identify an isolated portion which can be converted into an office, where you can work efficiently with least disturbances. It may even be a portion of your garage, attic, basement, loft or any other suitable area.

You have to ensure that all your non-office items from this area are either shifted somewhere else or utilised for the office - related productive activities. For instance, a box can be converted into a settee. **Nidhi Bakshi**, who is an interior designer operating from her home admits that even though her bedroom and bathroom are quite cluttered, she ensures that her "converted office" remains very clean and orderly to give the right impression to the clients.

There might be some lesser fortunate people who cannot have a separate identifiable place for the office. Don't despair. There are many possibilities of creating enough spaces for your office. Let us first begin by considering the basic requirements of the 'home office'.

REQUIREMENTS

For obvious reasons there are some essential requirements with a view to making your home office as comfortable as possible.

In addition to this, the office should also be convenient, functional, and professional.

Your office lay-out, decoration, size and location should be such so that it helps you in running your business efficiently. It is necessary that right at the outset you should work out the minimum requirement of the office space, its furniture, furnishings and other equipment. If you are going in for a high profile office, it is advised that you consult an interior designer and/ or an interior decorator to plan a suitable structure.

SELECTING THE RIGHT LOCATION

To select the best location:

- Carry out a space analysis in the whole house and examine as to where the required space can be made available. Do not leave out any structure or even open spaces in your house in this analysis. To that extent, basements, verandas, garages, niches and lofts, upper floors, sloping structures are also to be taken into account.
- Check up the open spaces adjoining your home to examine if a permanent/ temporary structure can be constructed to connect it to the main house so that a new structure along with some constructions within the house can be carved out to fulfill the office requirement.

- The same technique can also be used in utilising heights where an extension can be constructed by vertical separation. People have made mezzanine floors to create an additional floor for storage/ office space in their working area. Others have made modifications at heights to create lofts or erect overhead storage space to house cupboards or open racks. In some cases, when walls have sufficient thickness, appropriate cupboards or shelves can be made in the places where an in-built space can be carved out in the wall. The idea is to utilise every square inch of available space.
- A number of modern furniture companies can design furniture to suit the requirement of the proposed office. Others offer folding and/or extendible furniture. The possibility of installing sliding doors should also be considered as this helps in for creating more space. Illustrations in figures 1 to 8 may give you the necessary inspiration.
- The conversion or re-modelling at the aforesaid illustrations have been given to help you to decide on the best way to convert, re-design or re-model your office. Naturally, it will be depend on the layout of your existing dwellings. A number of people have room dividers in their drawing room or bed room, where they are big enough to create the office. As already stated, the majority have created an add-on annexe to the house and converted it into either an office or an additional storage room where the existing non-moving

Creating an Office in Home

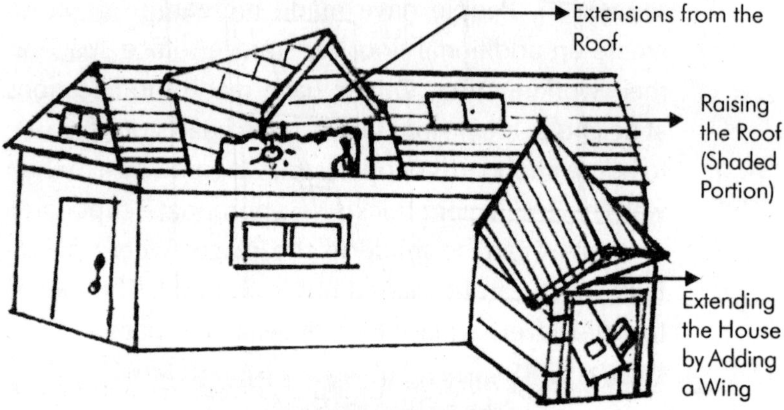

Figure 1: ADD-ONs for Office Spaces

Figure 2: Convert the Side Porch into an Office

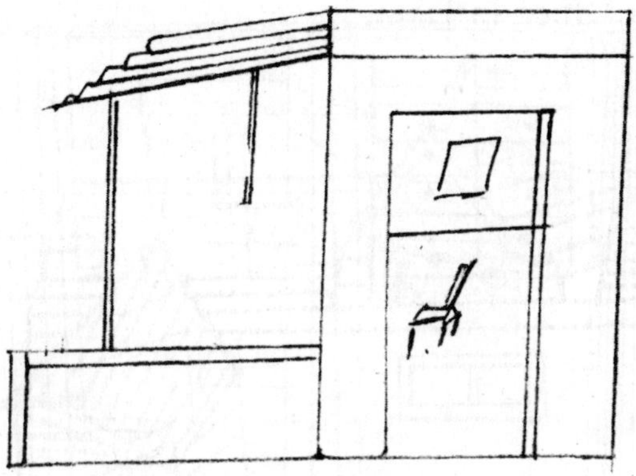

Figure 3: Semi-permanent Extension using Angle Irons, Poles and Roofing Sheets

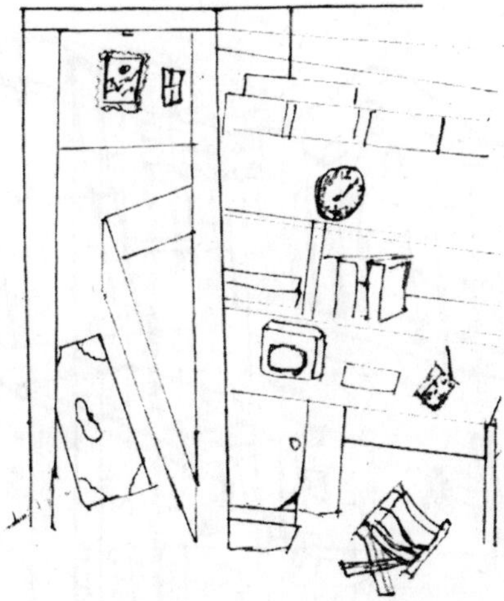

Figure 4: Partitioning a Large Bedroom to Create Office Space

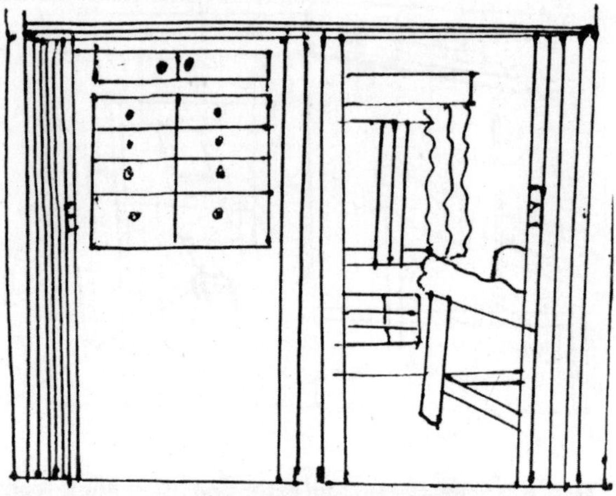

Figure 5: Accordeon Doors

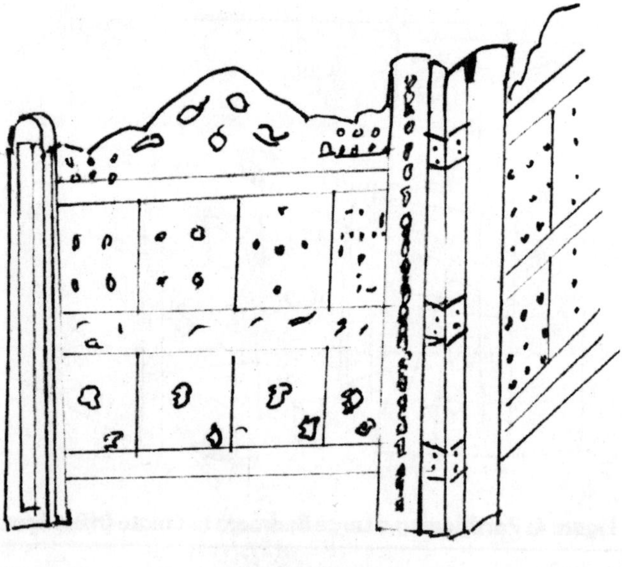

Figure 6: Screens

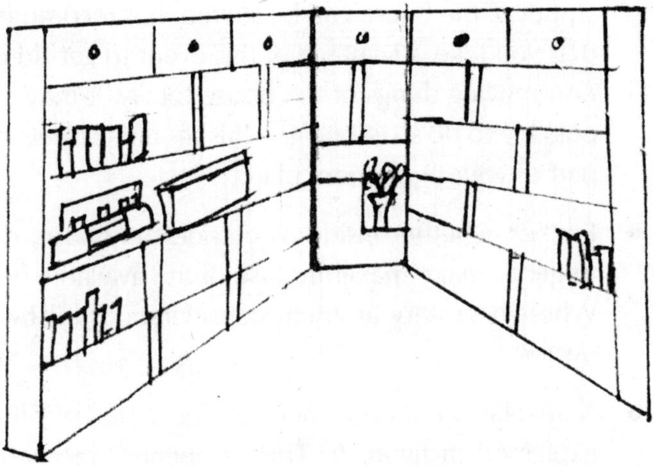

Figure 7: Wall Units Providing Additional Storage

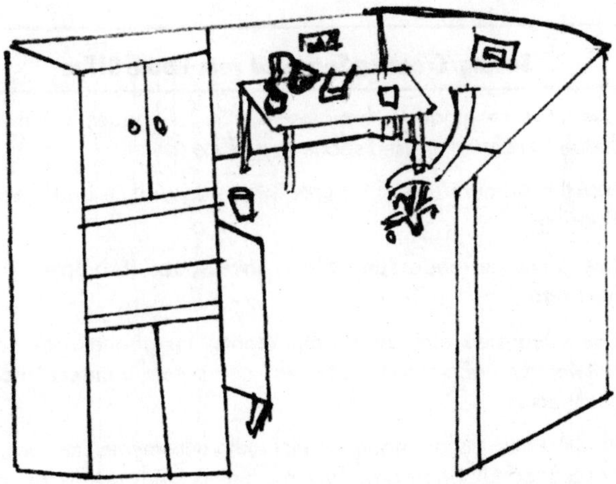

Panel

Figure 8: Panel Systems

clutter of the house can be shifted. It is recommended that you take advantage of this event to get rid of the non-moving things of the house totally. It may not be possible to do so in one go. This should, however, be a part of your permanent plan.

- Further, whether inside or outside the house, do not forget to make maximum use of the available height . Where necessary, aesthetic considerations will become over-riding.
- A special mention is needed for a boxed office as explained in figure 9. This, if opened, measures 64 inches but once closed measures around 32 inches x 20 inches x 45 inches only.

Saving/Creating Space for your Home Office	
1.	Use your imagination, brainstorm with colleagues, relatives and family to convert unused space into office space.
2.	Make maximum use of heights for storage/office and mezzanine flooring.
3.	Use products made specially to save space (Example – folding furniture).
4.	Use integrated electronic equipments, fax-phones, fax copiers, answering machines, telephones, computers, printers, modems, scanners etc.
5.	Review entire accommodation including basements, garages, attics, patio or porch, bedroom, drawing/dining, study rooms for creating the space required by you. You can also provide for, a) 'Add-on' space at different locations adjacent to the house or on roof tops.

Contd....

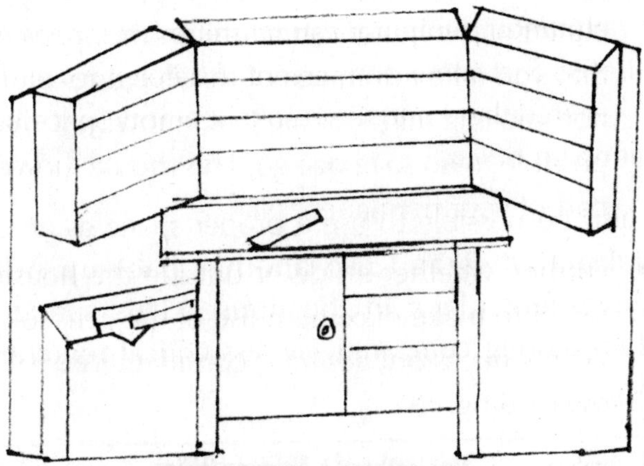

Figure 9: A Mobile Lockable Home-Office when Closed, could be just 33" × 21"×45"

b) A single, double or full dormer (projections built into steep roofs).

6. Review adjoining houses/flats to take them on hire for additional space requirements.
7. Having found the space, make an office suiting your work style e.g. private, compact with windows, shared or catering to your other personal requirements.
8. Remember, your office should be comfortable, convenient, functional and professional.

While working out the requirement of furniture and the office space you have to consider the requirement of space for files, computer, printer, telephone, fax-phone, fax-copier, scanners, modems and other equipment that might be necessary.

One should also examine if verandas and porches can be converted/modified for the purpose. It may also be possible to erect a permanent/temporary structure on the space adjoining the house, so that some non- essential belongings of the family could be shifted there and the resultant empty space be utilised for creating an office.

It may also be possible to use a proper space as an office for essential activities and use another back-up office at a less convenient place in the house. This space may be utilised for storing comparatively less critical requirements of the office.

The Looks of a Modern Office
Jimmy Mistry's firm 'Della Tecnica' is doing a brisk business of designing offices for corporates like Star TV, ANZ Grindlays, Emirates, Apollo Tyres and is a recent recipient of an award from Indian Institute of Interior Designers (IIID), Jimmy believes that a workplace must offer maximum productivity enhancement factors. The trend today is to go for simplicity, ergonomics, egalitarianism, using standardised, modular furniture using environment-friendly raw materials and conscious of employee safety. The colour and design of the office must make a statement on the image and organisational culture of the company.

Efficiency Tips

Other important tips for making your office appear more formal and efficient are as follows:

- Observe set working hours. You should let every one including your clients and family members know that you will be engaged in business activities during the specified time slots.
- Ensure that, if disturbed during the specified time slots, you tell the family clearly, but politely, that you

are working and are not available except in emergencies.

- If possible, close the office door/partition/room divider when you are working. If circumstances require it you can even hang a "do not disturb" sign on your office door.
- Locate your office away from the places, which are noisy. If possible, sound proof the office. Also try and have a separate office entrance for your visitors/ clients/ guests.
- Although you do not have to wear a coat or tie, dress yourself in a particular manner, which gives a clear signal to others that you are in a working mode and in a work attire.
- If possible, have a separate telephone for the office. Since answering machines are now available, use one for screening calls or receiving messages when you are not available.
- Be innovative in creating office space and in organising the office. Make use of space saving racks, mezzanine floors, filing cabinets, overhead lofts etc. for increasing space availability.

In important towns various hotels and business offices have separate rooms for business conferences. If you feel that your clients will not carry back a good impression of your home office you should try the option of hiring an alternative place.

COMFORT AND CONVENIENCE

In order to make it more convenient to your business, you might like to ensure the following as well:

- Tea/coffee/cold drinks should be available/offered to the visitors along with biscuits or light snacks, properly, formally and with finesse.
- If your home is difficult to locate, explain on telephone or send a letter indicating directions to your home.
- Keep the office bathroom absolutely clean and provide fresh toiletries. The office/offices and the bathroom must be neat, well painted/white washed and suitably lighted.
- Handle your friends and neighbours politely and tactfully with a view to convey that you would not like to be disturbed while working in the office.
- Approaches like "not now but when", may be used if contacted by people who might be keen to meet you.
- If you have some staff working with you, explain clearly the office arrangements and timings. It is necessary that you emphasise the need to have a formal relationship in the home office.

Finally, you also have to be alive to the security aspect of your home particularly if your business is bringing strangers inside it.

Some innovative alternatives may have to be devised to reduce visitors. **Ramesh Khanna**, a designer, made it a habit to pick up/deliver the art work to his customers, using a courier service.

The above stated measures would ensure that your work and personal life are separate even while you are working at your office located at your home. They will help you in your achieving the goal of keeping the boundaries of your home and office separate – in the minds and hearts of your family, relatives, neighbours and friends. Simultaneously, additional measures have been suggested to boost your business identity.

GROWTH PROBLEMS

Finally, if you find a need to expand the office space or staff due to the growth of your business:

a) Move to a bigger house.

b) Add on to your existing house.

c) Rent/buy an adjacent apartment.

d) Hire staff who can work from their own home.

e) Contract work with others businesses.

f) Rent a warehouse or storage or office space nearby.

g) Raise your prices.

h) Offer your business on franchise to others.

Needless to add that if you are only changing the form of the business without changing the concept of operating from home, all the other things which have been talked in this book remain relevant.

SELECTING THE OFFICE FURNITURE

People do not have a regular office accommodation at their homes. Even if you are lucky and you have an office, you will certainly not have appropriate furniture and furnishings for the office. This is on account of the simple reason that at the time of construction of the house your specific requirements of an office for the business you might start at a later date were unclear. It is therefore, necessary now to furnish your office suitably to make up for the inherent shortcomings.

The choice of the office furniture should indeed be very carefully made. One has to consider the requirements of efficiency, image and space. Considerable amount of sophisticated folding furniture is available in the market, which can be chosen for the purpose. There are special boards etc. which can be attached or encased in the walls. When required, they can be opened up to serve as tables or other platforms.

If you feel you will still be cramped, list out the furniture and fixtures at the house, categorise them at a rating scale from one to five and then use this scale to allocate/arrange the spaces. If you are cramped, some furniture/equipment, having low - priority, may have to even be disposed off or left out.

Many people do not exercise enough care and caution in selection of appropriate furniture. In their hurry to buy, they go and pick up from the market ill-fitting pieces. Remember, you have to use these pieces of furniture for a very long time. Your office chairs, tables and/ or desks, in particular, have to be selected with care.

A list of important furniture and other essentials is given in the next box. Whereas the tables/ desks are to be chosen, considering the space available and your other specific requirements, the chair should enable you to have a proper posture, a firm seat, arms and preferential requirements like adjustable height, foot-rests and tilt mechanism. If you prefer, they should also have rollers.

Important Furniture and Other Essentials	
1.	Pelmets and curtains.
2.	Lights - incandescent/fluorescent, tubes/pedestral table lamps.
3.	Desks - Appropriate width, depth & height, appropriate style.
4.	Chairs - Different styles including easy chairs.
5.	Tables - Work, conference, centre, peg, computer.
6.	Sofa and chairs.
7.	Book cases.
8.	Storage racks, mezzanine floors.
9.	Almirahs, cupboards, lofts.

In addition to the desk and chair you may also require items like couches, easy chairs, conference tables and chairs, central side tables, book cases, storage racks and filing cabinets.

LIGHTING UP YOUR OFFICE

Your aim should be to use as much natural light as possible and supplement the same with artificial lighting. The common types are incandescent and fluorescent lighting. The latter have the advantage of lower consumption of power and high lights. However, incandescent lighting reflects better on the skin and is gentler on the eyes than the fluorescent lights. The idea is to use the best combination to suit your requirements. Some lights may have to be hidden. Care therefore, has to be exercised in choosing the best combination of natural and artificial lights, hidden or direct.

CURTAINS

Your office may require curtains/blinds. Once again your specific requirements will come into play when you have to decide on curtains/blinds. In some other cases you might also like to go for sun- filming your window-glasses so that less sunlight comes in.

SOUND PROOFING

Sound proofing now-a-days is an important consideration. In addition to the curtains you may also have to go for thick carpeting, heavily padded furniture and wall panelling. If necessary thick insulation may have to be placed between the existing walls and the panels.

At times you may have to install your own sound system to keep alert and busy. This could be done through:

- A music system played softly.
- A cage of love birds or canaries. They chirrup and talk very pleasantly.

Such sounds will also help mask some of the outside disturbances, which cannot be eliminated by other measures.

MAINTAINING THE ADEQUATE TEMPERATURE

When you require to warm up your office, the following could be done.

- Have skylights and arrange your work area in the path of sunlight.
- Install solar panels to capture heat from the southern and western walls.
- Use room heaters.
- Add humidifiers to make the existing temperature warmer.

To cool off the office, the following can be done:

- Use fluorescent lights.
- Plant evergreens outside the walls on the southern and western fronts.
- Locate/place book cases on southern and western walls.

- Install window air-conditioners/coolers.
- Use blinds or curtains to block out direct sunlight.
- Tint windows which are receiving full rays of the sun.
- Use exhaust fans.
- Shut off appliances and lights when not in use.

The basic idea behind creating, designing, furnishing, lighting and decorating your office is that it should respond to your specific requirements considering your business needs. If possible, instead of making piece-meal purchases, the entire set of furniture and furnishings can be acquired at one go. If this is not possible, at least proper planning should be done so that articles subsequently acquired, fit/merge in the overall scheme.

Bargains Tips	
1.	See weekly classified advertisements under 'sale'
2.	Ask for business discounts
3.	Go for auctions
4.	In metro towns go for 'sale' at embassies or consulates.
5.	Look for people shifting or going abroad
6.	Buy good furniture with minor damages for a better bargain and get it repaired.

THE IMAGE OF EFFICIENCY

It is absolutely necessary that your office should not only give you an opportunity for operating efficiently but also should convey an impression of efficiency to the customers and visitors. Your filing system, should be an efficient one. All information must be available without delay from these files, whether they are manual or computerised. Using of proper cabinets or filing shelves is recommended.

If necessary, the floor and wall should be properly covered depending on your pocket and the image requirement. The floor should also be carpeted or covered with drugget/coir/durries. To give the impression of depth suitably selected paintings could be displayed in the space and waiting rooms. Suitable lighting, likewise, should be installed. People having small cramped places use big wall paper paintings on the wall to give an impression of the depth.

While designing an office we forget the fire and security requirements. Suitable fire extinguishers must be readily available and the electrical wiring should be properly secured to avoid any electrical fire due to short-circuits.

If necessary, a safe should be installed in the office wall. The possibility of installing burglar's alarms should also be examined. Depending upon the clientele, you are likely to receive, even a dog can be kept in the office. Some customers are scared of dogs and hence, necessary provisions for chaining them should be there.

The requirement of having a chowkidar who can sit outside the office needs to be considered. If the locality has a patrol system, you must also get your office listed in the beat.

Naturally it is expected that you will take measures to ensure that an adequate degree of cleanliness is maintained. The office must be swept/swabbed/dusted regularly to give a clean look. If there are bath rooms, they must have fresh towels, soaps, toilet-papers, odonil, other perfumes, etc. They (bathrooms) should be cleaned daily with phenol or any suitable substitutes. The seat should not only be very clean but should also give the impression of having been cleaned recently. A smell of Phenol or the cleaning item as well as a perfumed smell coming from the toilet (e.g. Odonil) gives the impression of neatness and order.

Similarly, to meet the requirements of drinking water, special mineral water or water purified through devices like acquaguard, coolers or Zero-B etc. should be catered for. The glasses in the offices should be spotlessly cleaned. If you intend to offer your customer tea or coffee and/or snacks, you must ensure that a good looking clean crockery is used. The biscuits should be dry and crisp. Even other eatable items should be fresh.

Finally, if you have a waiting room where your clients have to wait for sometime you must ensure that they are provided with some recent magazines and the day's newspapers. If need be, soft music can also be played.

Eco-friendly Measures	
1.	Use materials which can be reused and recycled.
2.	Buy products made of recycled paper
3.	Make pads from out-dated/used stationary

Contd...

4. Reduce AC load by reducing work during peak hot hours
5. Make use of internal fax in your computer
6. Use halogen fluorescent bulbs which produce more light and use less energy
7. Plant trees and have flower-pots
8. Avoid generating non-bio-degradable trash

So far, we have considered the requirements of creating, furnishing and maintaining the office. Let us proceed now to equip it suitably to make it an efficient functional outfit.

EQUIPPING THE HOME OFFICE

As stated earlier the reason behind the phenomena of more and more people opting for working from home is a tremendous boost in communication and information technology. Telephones and computers, combining with each other have contributed towards making the home office capable of meeting the requirements of any international firm. Even if you are planning to start your office with nothing more than a modest desk and the telephone extension, once you consolidate and start growing, you can suitably update your home office by keeping pace with the advanced technology. The range of new equipment and technology is likely to double or triple the personal capability, effectiveness and efficiency.

A modern office of today has at least one telephone, an answering machine, a personal computer, a printer, a photocopier, fax machine, modem and a number of other special telephone features. Fortunately with the cut-throat competition in the market for such equipment the prices are coming down all the time and the quality and capability of the equipment is going up. It is not necessary that you should buy all the above equipment. The acquisitions can grow gradually with the increase in the home business.

You can be sure that each of these additional features will add to your efficiency. Let us therefore examine in detail the kind of facilities which are likely to be available to you. With the fast rate of development and a breakneck competition there would be many more features and equipment available progressively for you. It is therefore, necessary that you keep in touch with the suppliers or their representatives/ agents for such facilities.

TELEPHONES

It is quite likely that, in India, telephone services will be privatised in the coming years, if they are not already by the time this book is published. Already a number of new models are appearing in the market, giving you a multiple choice. Remember it is the telephone which cuts down the distance between you and your business contacts. Our experience is that people working from home spend much more time on phone than on any other activity. Serviceable telephones at home will therefore be your prime KRA (Key Result Area).

Some of the special advanced important features which the modern telephones will be able to provide you are as follows:

- **3-Way Calling:** This permits you to talk to two other people simultaneously.

- **Conference Calling:** This will be more expensive and has to be arranged through an operator or a PCO (Personal Call Office). In this mode you can talk with a large number of parties at the same time.
- **Custom Ringing:** As per this feature you can have two telephone numbers of one line, each giving a different ring. The idea is to enable you to differentiate between established customers and others.
- **Automatic Number Identification (ANI):** This allows the person receiving a telephone call to see on a screen the number of the person making the call.
- **Call Forwarding:** This enables you to reach pre-selected people when you are not in the office.
- **Call Awaiting:** This gives you a signal of beep or click and the caller does not get a busy signal. This is possible when you receive the incoming calls while holding the original call.

Obviously the above features will be offered progressively by the telephone department or the private companies once privatisation is allowed. In certain cases where modem systems incorporating these features are available, it will be necessary for you to check the package of features they are offering and select the one which offers the best combination.

An important innovation on the telephone has been the introduction of cordless telephone as well as cellular phone. The cordless phone enables you to move around in your office. You have the facility of re-dialling the numbers, of storing important numbers in the memory, intercom capability between base set and hand set etc.

Innovative Services through Telephones

The Mahanagar Telephone Nigam Ltd. (MTNL), has been progressively acquiring a large number of innovative service packages and providing the same to their subscribers. Many more are on the anvil. These services shall be a big boon to the people who wish to work from home with minimal or nil over heads. A visit to their office in Delhi (Khurshid Lal Bhawan, Janpath) or Mumbai or the Internet site http://www.mc.in/mtnl or their directory on Internet at www.mtnlonline.com will give a very detailed information to the users.

With privatisation, even smaller towns will have the benefits of a vast array of services.

As far as the cellular phones are concerned they give you immense communication advantage since you can take them with you wherever you go. However, the price of the service is costly and hence, before you decide on having a cellular phone, it would be worth your while to undertake a cost-benefit analysis.

ANSWERING MACHINES

A number of answering machines have started appearing in the market. Acquiring and installing them, is a very good proposition. When you are away this machine gives a pre-recorded message and can take the message from the calling party. The only disadvantage so far is that technically they are quite prone to mechanical failure. While going through the brochures of these machines, it is recommended that you buy a make, which has a reputation for reliable performance.

PERSONAL COMPUTERS

Personal computers are invading homes at a fast pace and are becoming practically a normal feature of every home. The television extends your eyes, the telephone your ears and the computer does the same to your minds. If you are working alone you can have a quantum jump in your output. If you have a secretary you may not need additional staff. If you are working with a secretary and an accountant, they can do the job of 12 people of the office environment of yesteryears.

With the availability of personal computers at affordable prices it is strongly recommended that one should take maximum advantage of this facility. A number of software programmes are available for managing the information in your office, e.g. word processing, data base management, desk top publishing, pop-up programmes, personal information managers etc. Your computer dealer would be happy to advise you of the related advantages of each programme, so that you can use the best mix suited to your requirements.

While organising your computer files you must ensure that as far as possible the computerised system should correspond to the earlier manual system. To make your system effective, you should also do the following:

1) Use a utility that enables you to find your files.

2) Back-up contents of your hard disk on a floppy disk.

3) Erase back-up files which are not needed periodically, active files preferably daily and inactive files every month, to keep your disk uncrowded. Optimise your hard disk through a proper utility.

4) Use batch files to do routine and repetitive tasks automatically.

5) Store disks used frequently within your arms reach.

INTERNET

It is necessary that you become computer literate as quickly as possible. If you are not, you must be familiar with the Internet service and you should make use of these services. If you have a computer you can operate Internet from your home after meeting certain formalities. In India, your computer dealer will inform you how you can get the permission from VSNL after paying the required fee for Internet. Amplification and privatisation is already on the cards.

Internet has totally opened up access to information on a global basis while browsers, web sites etc., are fast catching up. Electronic mail is still the most valuable and growing Internet service amongst industrial and finance firms in India. Indeed e-mail is indispensable as it is a minimum cost, maximum benefit facility. These facilities can be used in all functional areas i.e., Operations, Productions, Marketing, Finance, Accounting,

Human Resources etc. Internet is used for searches beyond e-mail.

As stated elsewhere in the book, business to business electronic data inter change (EDI) has become an important part of infrastructure. These days this has reduced the time to complete a trail by 50%. The government has already framed rules of e-commerce (Electronic Commerce). It is extremely desirable to get familiar with the essential attributes of e-business.

Through EDI you can handle most of the paper work for transacting business like purchase orders, invoices, confirmation notices, shipping receipts at a lesser cost and better efficiency. It is basically the electronic transfer of commerce and administrative data from computer to computer using an agreed structure of the messages related to data items.

Protecting Yourself from Computer Hackers in the New Environment

Every time you access the Internet, you are exposing yourself to hackers anywhere in the world.

To protect yourself, pay attention to the following:

- People in the cyber space are not always what they appear to be. Never give your e-mail address to someone you meet in a chat room, a cyber-cafe or a on a bulletin board. He might be a prankster who will upload your C drive with all your data banks or may, out of fun, bomb your e-mail account.
- Do not down load programs to hear music, see pictures or get other features from websites you are not familiar with. You might down load a virus that erase your computer files, hijack your internet service, reconnect you to an international phone number, resulting in exorbitant telephone charges.

Contd...

- Once the PC bank account numbers are introduced by banks, be extremely careful to whom you give your financial or other personal information like credit card numbers or PC bank account numbers. A skilled hacker, even with partial information, can make unauthorised charges and deduct money from your account through the PC.
- For purchasing something on the Net, do not provide your payment information on-line. Do it by telephone or mail.
- Do not open e-mail, specially attachments, from an unknown sender. If, however, your curiosity gets the better of you, before you access any such mail, run an anti-virus software on your system.
- Refrain from distributing your e-mail address freely.

ACQUIRING A COMPUTER

It would be advisable to solicit a help and assistance of an expert, and at least a person familiar with computers to choose a computer system and software since there is a considerable obsolescence in computers. It is advised that you go in for an as modern system as possible which can be afforded by your pocket. You should also get a computer with a reputation for reliability.

If you are buying a used computer get it thoroughly checked by an expert. The most likely sources of problems with used computers are disk drives. Look out for an advertisement for 'computer melas' where special offers are announced.

Compare prices even in the same town. Try and persuade your employer, client or customer to buy a computer or give it to you on a hire purchase basis. Convince that this will be financially beneficial to him. If the requirement is low, rent a computer or peripherals with a colleague or a friend.

You will also have to buy a printer. Once again you will have to solicit your friends' help to select a printer with a reputation for reliability. It is advised that like the computer, you select a printer offering best quality of printing which fits within your budget. The printers are available in different models; starting from ink jet printers to the lazer jets with outstanding printing quality. Colour printers also available. Your pocket is the prime consideration.

MODEMS

If you can acquire a modem (modulator, demodulator) you can access a wealth of information which is on a computer. You can check stock price, conduct market research, investigate companies, find venture capital, recruit personnel etc. It enables you to transit information over the telephone lines via computer even faster than the fax machine at a low cost. Considerable amount of time and energy is saved by using modems. Once again we would advise you to acquire modems from a reliable company.

FAX MACHINE

Fax machine allows us to transmit data over telephone instantly to another fax machine or to a computer which is capable of receiving fax messages. Ever since the fax machine has come into business there has been a quantum jump in the transmission capability. The biggest advantage of fax machines is that they can transit total pages - typed, hand written or with figures/ sketches instantaneously. Thus, a garment buyer in London can communicate his preferred design to the manufacturer in

Ludhiana within seconds. The fax not only saves time but also cuts down the cost.

We could a use fax machine in several forms - one working inside a personal computer (PC) or as a totally independent self standing machine. The leading makers of fax machines are Canon, Panasonic, Ricoh, Toshiba etc. On account of competition in the market the prices are decreasing and technology is constantly improving.

It is advised that there should not be any compromise in the quality of paper used in the machine. Inferior paper will create problems.

PHOTOCOPIERS

If your business is likely to require a number of copies of the documents, you may consider going in for a photocopier also. A number of photocopiers are available these days with the suppliers giving the option of renting, buying or leasing the same. We would not advise you to buy a used photocopier. However, if it is necessary on account of cost consideration, it is better that you go for a "re-manufactured" copier which is being supplied from the factory where all the repairable/unserviceable components have been replaced.

FILING CABINETS

A number of alternatives are available for choosing an appropriate filing cabinet. Godrej, Remington and other major players will be able to supply you the required filing cabinet systems. It would be worthwhile for you to visit their showrooms in big towns to choose a cabinet matching your requirements.

VOICE MAIL

The time is not far off when a voice mail will be used as a regular communication feature in our offices. A voice mail turns a computer with a hard disk into a telephone answering machine – a phone mail system of a switch board. In fact it is a sophisticated answering machine that offers callers options beyond simply taking their messages.

It can take dictations, serve as an answering system as well as a phone book that enables one to call in and get phone numbers when you are away from home. However, it is not suitable for a small office. The biggest disadvantage of a voice mail system is that it uses a great deal of hard disk space.

The 'Electronic Home' is Coming

The dramatic change in the PCs from yesterday's number machining and word processing machines to today's globe spanning communications centre point out to the shape of things to come. The 'electronic homes' or 'e-cottages' are no longer a pipe dream.

The flexibility and efficiency of a home desk hot-wired to the one at work is increasingly appealing to employers and staff. For the home workers, who often have to contend with limited space, the arrival of integrated peripherals which combine several functions in one neat, compact package, will be specially welcome. Electronic giants like Sharp have already recognised the need for 'home offices' and are marketing average size units (E.9.F-3600M), which combine a laser printer with a fax, answering machine, scanner and photo copier.

Contd....

Technically, the most niggling problems with remote working are fairly simple ones, namely the incompatibility between different e-mail programmes and general office software. The psychological problems of isolated working and inability to run an 'office and home' at home are equally formidable. The answer to the latter lies is going through a learning programme as given in this book.

The concept of the electronic home or cottage is therefore likely to turn into a reality, fuelling many radical changes in the way we can earn a living. It certainly will result in a few giant steps towards the idea of working from home successfully.

GETTING THE BEST FROM YOUR EQUIPMENT

At Appendix 'A' a number of do's and don'ts as well as other optimisation techniques have been described to enable you to get the best out of telephones. It will be desirable if these are carefully studied to keep the cost low and efficiency high. Similar suggestions are given for PCs at Appendix 'B', printer at Appendix 'C' and fax at Appendix 'D'.

Having located, furnished and equipped your home office, let us proceed to study the issue of starting and managing the home office. This is described in chapter 6.

OOO

Appendix A

GETTING THE BEST FROM YOUR TELEPHONE

(1) Make STD and ISD calls in the concessional hours.

(2) As far as possible dial directly.

(3) Operator assisted calls take nearly 75% more time.

(4) If the privatisation of the telephone comes through, different companies will offer discounts for distance calls. Even now in India there are discount schemes for the callers wanting to make call to USA and other countries. Make use of these schemes.

(5) Always check your telephone bills for errors. It is not impossible that you might find mistakes, which can be subsequently rectified and credit obtained.

(6) It is more time saving to use touch and tone phones. The older rotary/dial phones take 4 to 5 times longer to dial a number.

(7) If you are very frequently dialling some numbers use the bills system in telephones including cordless phones where these numbers can be fed into the memory and dialling can be automatic.

(8) To reduce the expenditure, set up telephone appointments and agree on a particular time to call. On STD/ISDs, if the party has to be located and/or called from a distance, leave a message that you will call later at a specific time and disconnect and dial again at the indicated time.

Appendix 'B'

GETTING THE BEST FROM YOUR PERSONAL COMPUTER

You need a computer with the following minimum features-key board with comfortable keys, separate function keys, separate numeric key pad and separate cursor control keys.

MONITOR

While a monochrome monitor is suitable for most of the applications, colour is preferred by most of the people. You should be able to work on your monitor comfortably for many hours.

DISK DRIVES

At least one floppy disk drive and one hard disk drive capable of storing 40 MB should be available. Random access memory which stores a minimum of 6.0 K is recommended.

Ports: There should be at least two serial ports for communication-mouse and one parallel.

Service: It is preferable to have the facilities of site services.

Warranty: Although a number of assembled computers are available in the market we would advise you to get a reputed make having a 12 month or longer warranty. The credit card enables you to get a PC with longer warranty, but you will have to pay certain additional bank charges.

Appendix 'C'

GETTING THE BEST FROM YOUR PRINTER

- Select a printer which offers the best possible speed as well as quality consistent with your budget.
- Select a printer with a reputation for reliability.
- Select a printer which is consistently silent. Noisy printers are irritants to everyone and can affect your productivity. Ink jet and laser printers are quite silent.
- Check the repair/maintenance facilities. They must be very prompt.
- Memory should be adequate (not less than 512 Kilo bytes for a laser printer). In fact, more kilo bytes may be necessary if full pages of graphics are intended to be printed.
- In selecting a printer look out for signs of paper getting jammed. Paper jams are irritating and affect your productivity.

Appendix 'D'

Get the Best from Your Fax Machine

The resolution quality must be sufficient for your needs. If you are a graphic designer you will require a fax machine capable of higher resolution than most other businesses do.

The size of documents to be transmitted or received must naturally include all the sizes you require. For example ledger sheets may require a machine to take a relevant white paper document. A number of memory applications like automatic dialling, automatic retry or the document memory for despatch to multiple addresses are preferable.

Plain paper machines are more expensive while thermal paper fades. If possible acquire a fax machine with an automatic paper cutter. Other considerations are – buy the last year's model after ensuring that you will be able to get software and services for quite some time.

chapter 6

starting and managing the home business

Creating an office at home is as important as establishing proper work routines/systems and attending to your own self-management. These practices are necessary to enable you to run your 'Home Office' efficiently.

LEGALITY OF WORKING FROM HOME

Although working at home has been accepted for centuries, there are laws in certain places which prohibit you from using your home for business or commercial purposes. There are also certain products, which are banned for production within residential localities. There are also areas where no restrictions whatsoever are applicable. In others, a discrete home office is accepted provided it does not disturb the neighbours.

In many cases, an enlightened administration has laid down a number of exceptions to such laws as long as the office does not change the residential character of the building. If, therefore, the area where your house is located is prohibited from opening a business office one has to look a little further to check for concessions, which might be granted exceptionally.

Associations are repeatedly representing that these laws should be modified since they are outdated and are acting against the interest of the community. You also have to see the extent to which others in the locality are operating their businesses and what is the public acceptability factor. The way PCs are flooding the homes, a home office or an electronic cottage is popping up in practically every second house.

One important consideration is the activity which your business generates and the extent to which it can disturb the neighbours and community. Generally, people do not object a silent non-interfering activity in the neighbourhood. E.g. a pathological laboratory or a homeo clinic in the locality. Be as it may, it is for you to take the final decision. Even if some groups have represented to authorities about amending the rules and regulations you should understand clearly that, if the regulation prohibits a business activity, you may have to close your business once the authorities insist. No doubt, some authorities are lenient. But sometimes, due to changed circumstances or changed authorities, practices which were accepted earlier are rejected subsequently.

INITIAL FORMALITIES

Once you have checked the position and decided to establish your office you must ensure that all the formalities relating to the name, address, business etc. are complied with. These include:

- Deciding on a business name and if required registering the same with district/state authorities.
- If necessary, obtaining a business licence as well as a certificate of authority for sales tax purposes.
- Registering your firm with the post office for getting the necessary verification done by them for accepting the postal address, opening an account with the bank.
- Generally, the form of ownership adopted in such cases is a sole proprietorship. However, if one is going for a partnership or is floating a company, then the partnership deed or articles of incorporation, as the case may be, will have to be filed with the necessary authorities.

If you are using a trade mark for your firm, check up from the district authorities about registering the same with the district/ state concerned. For many types of businesses a trade mark is quite desirable.

It is also advised that you may either employ a lawyer on a monthly retainership basis or at least be in touch with him so that you can get the necessary help when required by you.

INITIAL PLANNING

Obviously you will have to plan for both long and short term. To start with, it is suggested that your long term may be restricted to a minimum of two years, while short term applies to an year or even six or three months. This goal is emphasised since working without a definite aim may result in gross under or over-utilisation of your potential. Once you have set your goals and converted them into tasks with relative priorities, you will have a reasonable idea if they are achievable. They might turn out to be very difficult or very easy to achieve and hence may have to be revised. Later, your planning cycle could be tailored to suit your working system. Once the picture is clear in your mind, write down your business plan under the headings described in the previous chapter. Many people are extremely reluctant to do this. Writing a simple business-plan and reviewing it periodically is an extremely helpful step for your business.

The next step would be to set up a proper system so that your office can work most efficiently. Obviously this will be related to the business requirements and domestic environment. These aspects have been dealt with in succeeding chapters.

We would also like you to adopt a flexible approach in the beginning later on so that you can modify your working system easily and quickly. However, you should be able to have a firm system suitably tailored to meet your business requirements.

At the box below, twelve critical decisions have been listed, which are necessary for starting and managing your office effectively. Do refer to them from time to time to check if you are on the right track.

Twelve Critical Decisions in Managing your Office at Home

There are 12 critical issues, which you will have to address, find answers to and incorporate in your working routine. These are:

1) What will be your working hours? No. of hours/days during the week? Holidays? Off-days?
2) Weekly visit schedules to your clients/ customers?
3) Breaks, including those for lunch, tea/coffee and snacks. How many & when?
4) When will you be available to your family during the day? You should also specifically fix- time slots in the week for doing house-hold chores.
5) What will be your office clothes?
6) How much and when will you watch T.V.? What other work you will do while watching T.V.?
7) How will you manage your working finances? How will you manage your emergency requirements?
8) What interruptions you can allow during your office work?
9) What additional help you are likely to require immediately or later?

Contd....

10) If the requirement exists, then, when will you recruit, train and induct people?
11) What will be your vacation time? Under what circumstances will you take an additional day or part of the day off e.g. morning, afternoon or evening?
12) What regular information is required to be maintained up-to-date by you or to be kept track of?

INSURANCE

You may not realise but operating efficiently from home can increase your assets by as much as Rs. 25,000 to Rs. 1,00,000 or even more. You must insure these assets adequately against fire or theft. It is also to be remembered that if your vehicles or premises are being used for commercial purposes they need to be covered adequately by an additional insurance.

It is necessary that you protect yourself against the likely risk to yourself as well as to your business assets. In this connection, what is heartening is that a large number of innovative insurance schemes are coming up and these should be taken advantage of. It would be also advisable to keep in touch with your insurance agent so that you can be aware of new kinds of policies, which may be introduced in future.

The insurances which you should have are as follows:

- Personal health insurance and/ or mediclaim.
- Insurance of business property in the home office.

- Auto insurance, if vehicles are used for commercial purposes this may include the vehicles carrying company goods to outside destinations.
- Disability insurance, if available in your town. This is a new scheme which is being talked about, where in case of more than 90 days of disability, one is likely to get the necessary help from insurance.
- Home insurance.
- Insurance against interruption.
- Insurance of employees in the office.
- Partnership insurance.
- Insurance against claims, suits related to your product or service.
- Life insurance.
- Special computer insurance if required or considered necessary.

Presently, all insurances are in the hand of public sector insurance companies. But the time is not very far when private insurance companies are likely to step in. If you are getting an offer of an insurance package from an insurance company located outside your state, check and ensure that the company is authorised to do business in the state in which you are located.

TAX BENEFITS

Generally, the income tax authorities accept your conducting a business from home. In some cases they insist upon the fact that your home office should be a separate office within your residential premises and should be used "exclusively" and "regularly" for business. In some cases e.g.. lawyers, doctors, management consultants etc., may be allowed deductions for seeing clients at home. This may be permissible even when the place of business is located somewhere else. It is always desirable to check with an income tax consultant regarding the tax benefits you are likely to obtain from the government. Some of the possible home office expenses worth trying for claiming deduction are given below:

- Depreciation of home (partial).
- Maintenance/cleaning of the home office.
- Household furniture converted for business office.
- Household supplies used for business office.
- Property tax (partial).
- Rent paid if you rent a lease (partial).
- Telephone.
- Utilities attributed to business.

There are also a number of deductable business expenditures, which could be claimed in your tax returns. These are:

- Accounting and book keeping fee.
- Fee for legal retainership.
- Some advertisement expenses.
- Car expenses including Automobile Association membership, rent for garage and losses on sale of, cars.
- Business starting up expenses.
- Business seminars, business meals, bad debts, bank service charges etc.
- Books and magazines, copyright costs, consultant costs for reducing costs of business, capital expenditure, commission paid to agents and sales representatives.
- Depreciation on other equipment.
- Professional and trade association dues.
- Clubs and fraternal organisations.
- Travel expenses for management development.
- Electronic mail services.
- Furniture and equipment for the office.
- Insurance expenses.

- Licence fee and taxes.
- Courier services.
- Office supplies.
- Losses in previous year/years.
- Expenses for incorporation.
- Fees for passports.
- Travel agency payments.
- Repair/maintenance of business property.
- Travel expenses.
- Gifts limited to a specified amount per recipient per year.
- Postage.
- Retirement/pension contribution.

When choosing your income tax Consultant, you must ensure that you are selecting a person who has sufficient experience in preparing tax-returns and he has been appearing for the income tax appeals. If possible consult your other business friends and colleagues.

Clear and complete records of your income, assets, expenses and liabilities must be maintained by you or your accountant to enable you to file tax returns as well as obtain proper reductions. Unless you are very good at preparing your own tax return, we shall advise you to obtain the help of professional to do so. Further, do keep checking on the grant of additional deductions, which become permissible from time to time.

MANAGING THE INFORMATION/ CORRESPONDENCE

If one compares the situation as it exists today compared to the situation a decade ago, it will be clear that there is virtually a flood of information, messages, letters etc. for each person, particularly those engaged in business. If one does not process this information quickly, file it, as well as dispose off the unwanted stuff regularly, he will soon find important letters, business cards or other important documents etc. misplaced. This, in fact, could also be termed as missed opportunities. There are instances when a person has to go through these files and papers to search for important documents and only locate them after a few hours' search.

The golden rule is, "everything in its place and a place for everything". In other words, unless a paper is destined for the waste paper basket, your filing system must ensure that it goes to the relevant file and there is a reliable indexing to locate that file when it is required. Even computer users suffer from this problem. Many a times they forget what they named the file as or in which disk or directory they have put it in. This is as serious as misplacing an important enclosure in a memo or manual file folder.

It is therefore, important for your business to have a proper system for processing and managing the information received by you through different communication media, so that the same becomes available when it is needed. Your indexing system should be such that no time should be lost in locating a particular file or paper.

FEATURES OF AN EFFECTIVE FILING SYSTEM

An effective filing system should have the following features:

a) A proper routine for receipt, processing, storage and despatch of the information.

b) A proper indexing system indicating, where the information would be available.

c) A periodic and convenient time drill to file the incoming communication.

d) A back up system to make storing and locating of the information very convenient.

e) A system for rejecting and getting rid of the information which is of no use.

REQUIREMENTS OF A PROPER FILING SYSTEM

A file is an enclosure where all related enclosures pertaining to one particular aspect of the work are filed. The most important use of a file is to maintain the related documents pertaining to a subject and to facilitate retrieval of these documents when required without delay.

A file could be on a project, an order, a client/ customer or any other subject, but as stated earlier it should contain the essential related information on that subject or sub-subject.

The essential principles of a good filing system are as follows:

1. A place for everything and everything in its place.
2. All incoming correspondence, which needs to be retained should be filed immediately with proper cross-reference. (In this connection do remember our advise of utilising your leisure time (watching T.V. etc.) for sorting out your papers and filing them.
3. Enclosures should be filed in chronological order, duly cross referred.
4. All unnecessary paper clips should be removed before filing.
5. There should be an index of files, e.g. 'C'/1 Contract Correspondence, Policy, 'C'/1/1 Contract Correspondence with M/s. Sahu Packers Ltd.' All files should be properly labelled.
6. Files should not become bulky. Check your files periodically for rejecting the outdated enclosures.
7. Reduce legal and bulky documents to small sizes for easier filing.

8. Keep a 'tickler system' where there are 31 separate cards for each day of the month and details of a particular file required on a particular date are noted down in advance on these cards. On review of the card of the day, the file to be put up can be taken out.
9. Important information/statistics can be displayed on planning calendars, bulletin-boards, black-boards, white boards and other materials which are available in the market.
10. Filing system can be supported by business card folders. Like files, the cards must be regularly reviewed to ensure that outdated/obsolete/unwanted cards are removed.

MANAGING IN THE HOME OFFICE ENVIRONMENT

An appropriate system is a necessary prerequisite for an efficient home office management. The system should take care of your work routine, your self-management and management of relationships at home.

P.K. Khanna, a successful businessman working from his own home office describes his routine like this, "I get up at 5 in the morning, make my own tea and go out for jogging. After returning, I have another cup of tea with my wife, and get ready for the office. From 8 to 9 a.m., I make my telephone calls and then have breakfast. Then I am back again into the office to attend to my business. I have afternoon siesta for a couple of hours and get out thereafter to meet my clients. Every Monday morning I pay my bills and update my books/records".

There are others who have their own way for organising their work, managing their time and managing their relationships with the wife and children at home. Most of them exhibit the following traits:

- Good self organisers, in control of their activities, they are always on the lookout for improvement in their schedules to increase productivity.
- They develop the knack to clearly identify their goals and objectives, classifying them as urgent or important or routine and then creating a system around these tasks to achieve the goals within deadlines.
- They structure their time comfortably, at times planning months/weeks ahead to cater for all foreseen requirements, e.g., outstation visits, family gatherings and vacations, etc. This gives them enough cushion for planning routine work as well as for tackling unforeseen problems.
- Good self-managers are also fairly flexible so that depending upon the task requirements they can organise their time involvement. Thus, if an important task has come which requires their total involvement, they ensure that a bulk of the time is set apart for the task exclusively.

They carry out an evaluation of their SWOTs (Strengths, Weaknesses, Opportunities and Threats) from time to time to make changes in their business, organisations, operations and working routines. They are aware of how far they must go and take decisions accordingly.

In particular, they:

1) Set realistic and attainable targets for important objectives in terms of time, money and other resources.

2) Allow adequate buffers for unforeseen events which will cause delays.

3) Set their objectives in terms of specific results to be obtained.

4) Review major objectives on a specific date every month. Only if it absolutely warranted do they change the objectives.

5) Write their objectives on a calendar or pad, which can be checked regularly.

6) Arrange the objectives in the order of priorities.

7) Create routines for monitoring the objectives. For example, one may decide to review the progress everyday when going for a long morning walk.

8) Develop proper information linkages.

9) They are in touch with the right people who can provide new and latest information all the time.

10) Ensure regular and adequate cash generation for carrying out their business from home. This involves a vigorous follow-up of recovery of receivables.

11) They are never short of "working capital". They review their financial position from time to time and ensure recovery of outstanding dues.

12) They insist that goods or services being delivered by them conform consistently to the required quality.

13) They make sure that all their assets are fetching reasonable earnings and you are making consistent efforts to earn money from the non-earning assets. Depending upon your liquidity, this can be a factor which can help you dramatically while you are trying to get organised. If you have an idle resource, whatever it may be, e.g. your time, place, entire house, part of the house, machines/computer, manpower, vehicle etc., always check if the same can be hired out for adequate returns. Develop a culture so that your staff are also encouraged to innovate in all the activities of the business. Reward the staff through cash or kind whenever the business makes significant gains. Reward yourself too.

14) Communicate, don't commute, unless it is necessary for the business. Whenever you have a choice, use the telephone/fax to save valuable time.

15) Also keep in mind that you do not become home-oriented introverts. Some calls to important people/

customers are necessary as part of their duties to maintain necessary/vital contacts for business.

16) Are flexible. Although disciplined working is highly desirable, they do not make the system so rigid that it cannot be changed to meet emergencies. Do change at times, but, do revert back to the original system as soon as possible.

17) They ensure that no time is wasted and meetings/ conferences, visitors and interruptions are properly organised. Do refer to the detailed guidelines on managing your time effectively at box below for important tips .

Mastering Time Management

- Appreciate the importance of your and others' time.
- Retrieve/save as much time as you can from daily activities.
- Ensure best utilisation of time and do things in time.
- Analyse time utilisation to retrieve/save as much time as possible.
- Plan your daily, short-term and long-term activities.
- Organise office working effectively, make the best use of telephones, manage visitors, interruptions, meetings and discussions for maximum time saving.
- Make the best use of your best time. (knowing your body cycle use your best time, when you are most alert, for your most challenging activities.)
- Develop your profession, career, relationships, health mental faculties and spiritual accomplishments in a balanced manner. This will ensure availability of maximum time for the business while maintaining a healthy and alert routine.

Contd....

- Generate time. When seeing a TV serial, travelling by flight, train or visiting a dentist etc., where you are likely to be delayed, take additional work which is pending or books/magazines to read.
- Review your pattern of time spending every three or six months. Identify time wasting habits, which unobtrusively creep in without your noticing them.

WATCH OUT FOR NINE DEADLY TIME STEALERS

1. Television
2. Longer & more frequent breaks
3. Visiting friends, neighbours/relatives, over-socialising
4. Long telephonic conversations
5. Starting late, stopping early
6. Worrying but not doing
7. Prolonging/concentrating on less important tasks
8. Day dreaming, planning a glorious future
9. Falling sick frequently.

Identifying and Tackling the Deadly Time Stealers

On the first day of every month, examine all the points mentioned above one by one and identify your current major time stealers. A mere self-investigation itself would pave the way for you to conserve time. You can also resort to the following:

1) T.V.: Select only a few programmes during the day/ week for watching. If you can do another activity or a couple of additional activities alongwith watching the programmes, so much the better. For e.g. you can read/ scan a business article while watching the T.V. serial. It will be an ideal fit.

2) Talk to yourself about the need to cut down time spent on non-productive activities, whether telephonic talks to your friends or visiting them. Set a timeframe for each of these activities.

3) Remember, the best photograph is of no use in the camera if its reel is not taken out and developed. Tell yourself repeatedly to initiate the process of "doing it".

4) Set up specific rituals for starting your daily work, finishing the same or going to meeting people etc. For example, you could change to semi-formal clothes for going to your home office and wishing your wife a good-bye loudly and clearly. Similarly, at the close of the day associate the closure of the daily activities with a specific action e.g., taking a small walk or going to the children's room etc.

LAABH HI LAABH

Commandments for Effective Time Management

- **Time - A daily Miracle:** One of the prime resources of an entrepreneur or manager is his time. It is a daily miracle, yet unlike your other important resources e.g. money, you cannot accumulate it to spend it later on an appropriate occasion.
- **Have sound Values, Principles and Goals:** Gradually time planning has to become part of the life planning. Try to acquire sound values, principles and goals to progress with least complications and minium overall wastage of time. Values are the stars you can use for navigation in the darkest of nights when no other aids are available. Principles are guidelines for specific action at all time. Goals give you a purpose and a plan.
- **Review your time ultilisation Periodically:** Analyse and put your time utilisation under a microscope periodically, say on the first week of every quarter. Don't be shocked to find your time involvement with some mundane activities to be too high. Bad habits creep in quietly like the camel in the tent and settle down permanently in your system. Identify them to eliminate them. Too much time in reading of newspapers, watching TV, eating, over-socialising, phone calls, meetings, conferences/ seminars, visitors, interviews etc. need to be controlled tactfully. Learn to say 'No' politely but firmly.
- **Daily Planning:** Daily time planning before the start of your work is an absolute 'must'. Keep a card in your pocket listing your tasks for the day. Dovetail these tasks with weekly, monthly or quarterly tasks. Prioritise the tasks as vital, essential or desirable. The day should be a mix of planning and execution. Remember, it is equally necessary to regularly mend your nets when you are not fishing.
- **Delegate:** Select and develop subordinates to delegate tasks and responsibilities leaving you to perform the functions appropriate to your level. Watch out for 'Upward Delegation' by extra-smart subordinates which results in their playing golf or cricket during the weekend while you are busy at home doing 'their work. Do not be a perpetual perfectionist. Be selective. Train yourself to look the other way at times.
- **Organise Yourself and Your office Work:** Carefully control telephone calls, visitors, interruptions and meetings to save time. Make sure that your documents are filed on the principle 'A place for everything and everything in its proper place'. So many times managers are found looking for hours for an urgent paper filed at a wrong place. Try and deal with one paper/mail only once. Cut down superfluous words in e-mails. Ensure that your office becomes a platform for effective action, while simultaneously ensuring that it does not become a 'watering hole' of gossips and time wasters.

* By R S Shukla 'The Times of India' 22-02-2001.

LAABH HI LAABH

Some more Commandents for Time Management

- **Cheat the System to Get more out of your Time:** While watching TV, waiting for a flight, travelling in a car or a train, waiting for an appointment e.g. with a bureaucrat, doctor or dentist, do one or two additional useful things alongside to utilise your time productively.
- **Be a 'Wait Watcher':** Read a report, an article, or a book or take on some other useful task. Think about some problems when you are on your health jog/walk. Certain international airports provide facilities to operate laptops.
- **Make 'Best' Use of your 'Best' Time:** The trick is to do your most creative challenging thing when your system is ready to take on the toughest job. Examine your body clock to identify your time zones to do things prioritised on the ABC scale. An early riser can work 'A' tasks in the morning just as the night owls can do the same in the nights. Try and accommodate.
- **A 'Balanced' Growth Helps to provide Maximum Time:** In the long run, maintaining a proper balance in working for a career, nurturing relationships, keeping a good health, and consistently improving mental and spiritual accomplishments will make you a stronger person and will make maximum time available for productive work to you. Sacrificing everything else for a brilliant career is a self-defeating exercise.
- **Contribute to the Total Organisation Time:** Success of an organisation depends not only on the senior executives being able to put in long hours, but maximising in the availability of 'Total Organisational Time' of the entire personnel. Ensure that the seniors, peers and subordinates are not kept tied down inordinately affecting their performance. Appreciate the value of your time as well as that of others.

SIGNS INDICATING THE NEED TO REORGANISE

A sure indication that your system needs reorganisation is given by the following signs:

1) Not having time for doing important things. Postponing tasks, experiencing overcrowding of activities.
2) Haphazard keeping of books, files, notes, magazines, newsletters etc.

3) Spending too much of time everyday on locating important documents.

4) Missing appointments/deadlines.

5) Feeling that things are getting out of hand.

6) Finding overdue bills among other papers or important letters for which action should have been taken earlier.

7) Being uncertain about your bank balance.

8) Too many interruptions.

If the above signs have started appearing regularly in your system it is clear that you need a better system to get things back under control. Review and reorganise immediately.

DEVISING A PROPER WORK SCHEDULE

1) Structure your schedule to fit your work pattern. For example, if your clients are likely to drop in during the afternoon or evening you should settle appointments in those time slots only.

2) Recognise the body cycle relevant to the activities which are most complex during your most creative time. This will be different with different people. There are some people who sleep late in the night and get up late while others who are early sleepers and early risers. Your routine should be tailored around your

specific productive times. Likewise, some of us wish to have a siesta after lunch. Do cater for it in your schedule, if you feel it is desirable.

3) Set up a proper schedule. Gradually you can modify the schedule around other important priorities of your life. Do ensure that business does not adversely affect relationships, physical fitness, acquiring knowledge regularly and other essential routines like meditation, yoga etc. A large number of people are fond of going for morning walks. It will not be advisable for them to give up the walks. Rather, it will be advisable to combine the walks with some other activities like daily planning, networking, praying etc.

4) At the beginning you may have to carry out a review of your schedule very frequently, but once the routine is established try to do it at least once in three months.

Steps for Optimising Efficiency

1. Plan your month, week and work day. If necessary planning may extend beyond a month. You may like to use a yearly planning calendar for this.

2. Allocate buffer time for unforeseen activities.

3. Set objectives and goals and review progress regularly.

4. Take frequent breaks to introduce variety.

5. Never give up extra curricular activities.
6. Pat yourself on the back for completing important tasks.
7. Display/forecast key activities. If needed, these can be displayed on the white board or an aide-memoire pad placed on your table.
8. Review all current activities to examine that you are not devoting more time than what is necessary to some of them.
9. Keep an eye on the time spent and calories consumed during the meal/snack breaks or visits to the refrigerator. Many home based businessmen have complained that they put on too much of weight within the first six months on account of change in life style. Others discover that their durations of breaks have increased beyond limits.
10. Learn to say "no". This should be done firmly and politely and, if possible, with an offer of alternatives. This will convince the other party that you have a genuine problem.
11. Do more than one thing at a time.
12. Plan a project during your work. Listen to an information/ tape while shaving, scan magazines while watching T.V. etc. Read books/magazines during journey by air/rail.

13. Communicate, do not commute. What can be handled by phone or by post should not be done by making unnecessary visits and wasting valuable time.
14. Stay cool. Never get annoyed or angry. In the final analysis, the person who gets annoyed is the worst loser.
15. Always believe in the magic of accomplishing big jobs by taking small steps one at a time.
16. Take a deep breath or a 5 minutes break or count 1 to 10 if you feel that you are being rushed.
17. When under stress tell yourself that this too will pass like so many other things.
18. Encourage yourself, using aphorisms like "just do it" or "when the goings get tough, the tough get going", etc.
19. Smile and laugh, even when things are not going smoothly.
20. Always be on the lookout to change your complex work into simple routine system. For instance your, mail can be seen once or twice during the day and not as soon as it is received.
21. Be enthusiastic and cultivate zest for your work.
22. Always have a sense of timing in what you do. A thing done, the way it is done and the time taken for doing it are of relevance.

23. Avoid perfectionism everywhere. Even the 'American Charter of Independence' drafted by Thomas Jefferson and hailed by the world as one of the most wonderful written documents had a number of spelling mistakes.

How to Ensure that You Don't Overwork or Become a Workaholic

It is necessary for you to achieve a balanced application of work, maintenance of relationships, personal health (including exercise, rest & relaxation), intellectual and spiritual pursuits simultaneously. Most of these can be attended to if you plan your routine properly e.g.. you can plan your vacations even 2-3 years in advance. There would also be shorter breaks, attending meetings, ceremonies, visiting relations etc. This also can be indicated in your table dairy/calendar/planning calendar in advance.

You must give yourself a holiday once a week besides giving distinct breaks everyday as well. Goad yourself to get out of the house once every week (In addition to getting out and meeting people, which is your official obligation).

If, despite the above you find signs of over working, the inescapable conclusion is that you have a tendency of becoming a workaholic, which, if allowed to grow, will eat eventually into your own productivity and success output. Under these circumstances, it is necessary that you appreciate the following points.

1. Rest and relaxation are necessary for increasing your efficiency and productivity.

2. There is a difference between over work and hard work. Slow and steady hard work with breaks of rest and relaxation will bring you more stimulation than an obsessive tension filled routine.

3. Note your minimum and maximum. Learn to say "no" when you are approaching the maximum limit. Do not hurry too much. Try your best or try not to be perfect. Look for alternatives including delegation of your work to someone else or reducing it.

4. Above all, make sure that you utilise your leisure hours fully doing the things you like best. In other words, you must pamper yourself.

5. Remember, if you do not change your track, you may be heading for a 'job burn-out' or a 'nervous breakdown' or ulcers or a heart condition - none of these will do any good to your health or for that matter to your business.

ESSENTIALS OF 'WORK FROM HOME' AGREEMENT

In case of a regular job being done at home for your employer, it is preferable to have a formal work-from-home agreement with him. Essential elements of this agreement can include the following:

1. Salary/wages, methods, periodicity, review, increases, fringe benefits, medical, compensation, insurance.

2. Minimum time and when to be at office.
3. Tasks/targets, performance evaluation, task completion.
4. Materials, resources, equipment requirements.
5. Training & promotion opportunities.
6. Notice period for termination and other modalities if required.
7. Possibility of returning to work at the office, if required.

You have now been briefed adequately on how to start and manage your home office efficiently with some critical self-management advice since you are the most important resource in your home venture. Let us now move over to other key areas which contribute critically to your business performance from your home office. The most important amongst these are marketing and financial management.

ooo

chapter 7

marketing functions

People tend to neglect marketing, more so when they are very confident of their product or service. Don't ever go by your exclusive perception of saleability of your product. Rather, go methodically on a market survey and then develop your four Ps, i.e. product, price, promotion and place or distribution. See if you can acquire some personal experience in marketing of your proposed product with someone else. Above all, as a home-based person, have a definite target of visiting and/ or calling on phone a minimum number of customers every week.

ESSENTIALS OF MARKETING

Marketing and Financial Management are the main props of any business. Someone has rightly stated that while finance is the breath for the corporate body, marketing is the daily food. If you think, you can survive without appropriate marketing, try and imagine what will happen to your business if you had no buyers for a few weeks.

The important things to be remembered while planning your marketing strategies for the home business are as follows:

Absolute Need for Market Survey Prior to Launching your Business

It is not enough to have a good and proven product or service. The business scene is full of examples of brilliant engineers who have produced outstanding products, but failed in business because they either ignored or were over confident of the marketability of their products. An **ex-garment factory** manager producing garments for more than 5 years announced a seminar on garment export without even consulting a handful of garment managers in the field. The fact was that the timing and duration of participation of the seminar were unsuitable for the organizations who were busy with their export commitments. The result was a very poor participation in the seminar, which was outstanding in terms of course content, faculty and utility.

The organiser of the seminar suffered a major loss because he forgot to take the basic marketing step of checking whether the product was acceptable to the market, at the time and for the duration which was being charged. He lost a considerable amount of money because he was over-confident of his success. Even at the risk of sounding repetitive we would like to emphasise that a proper marketing survey must be conducted prior to launching your business. The survey findings must have a virtual influence on the four Ps of your marketing i.e. product (or service), price, promotion and place.

Using your Immediate Past Experience/ Relationships

In a number of cases, people having a job develop close relationships with the client organisations. It is easy for them to shift to their own home office and independently operate from home. They have the advantage of committed clients as well as of offering the services at a lower price on account of low overheads.

Amit Chopra, a Computer Engineer, was working with a prestigious firm. After nearly 5 years of working with the firm, he had cultivated healthy relationships with a number of major buyers. He shifted to his own home-based business and continues to do very well. He had already earned the confidence of his customers. All he needed was to maintain his credibility and good rapport with clients.

Target Market

It is always good to select a specialised 'niche market' to serve from which you can draw the business you want to. This ensures that the time and money spent on marketing is reasonable. **A.K. Aggarwal** uses this approach when he advises different firms on their procurement strategies and operations. He had cultivated these firms prior to his leaving the job and taking on consultancy.

Outstanding Marketing Professionals

Many marketing professionals have pursued multi-disciplined marketing techniques, which range from exhibitions/ trade shows, networking, brochures, advertising, seminars, marketing through direct mail etc. and have been successful in getting the good business for their products/services. These are people who are outstanding in networking and in aggressive marketing. In fact, when the business scene becomes grim they are the ones who are sought out for help by the beleaguered firms. You could consult these people before launching your business.

Positioning Yourself as an Important Person

People acquire reputation by virtue of their field experience or achievement in their work. e.g.; writing articles in journals, books or any similar important achievement. If you have such a capability, it will be worthwhile highlighting that you are recognized and accepted as an important authority on the subject. Other ways to promote yourself are given in the box below.

Different Ways to Promote Yourself	
◆ Teaching classes	◆ Appearing on cable network
◆ Speaking in seminars	◆ Distributing brochures and fliers on yourself,
◆ Advertising in local papers	◆ Being active in social activities, clubs
◆ Donating and volunteering	◆ Putting up banners and posters
◆ Distributing samples	◆ Joining professional organisations
◆ Talking to people on phone	◆ Giving speeches
◆ Writing articles	◆ Networking at social events etc.

Acquiring A Marketing Approach

Many of us are not really suited for marketing functions. Yet, with little effort one can develop a proper marketing mindset. This can be done through a step-by-step approach by doing the following:

1) Identify your target markets and try and know as much as possible about them, e.g., retired persons of high income group in Noida.

2) Find the best way to let your markets know your business and then follow up with a proper positioning strategy.

3) Practice positioning your product and service by describing your product/service in 25 to 30 words, giving the most important features. Practice doing it with your prospective clients.

4) The product or service provided by you should give the customer pleasure, profit and confidence. In other words, instead of going just for selling, you should strive for obtaining the customer's delight.

5) The above strategy to identify the market and the ways to deliver total customer delight will change your mindset gradually and make you a marketing person.

Marketing Information

Develop a system of obtaining all the relevant information on important marketing inputs, competitive situation, suppliers, buyers and on the likely competition in future - be it the product, service, competitors, technology, price, distribution systems, advertising, other promotion techniques, etc. Contribute to journals and become a member of useful groups, associations.

MARKETING METHODS

As explained earlier, a number of strategies could be employed to launch your home business. Generally, it has been our experience that, amongst alternatives available for marketing in the business, the most expensive alternative may not be the most effective one. Advertising, direct mail and despatch of customised information to likely clients is very effective. However, you being the person on the spot have to decide on the best course of action. There are a number of alternative methods, which could be adopted either in isolation or in combination with others. These are as follows:

1) **Creative Advertising:** Creative advertising enabling good positioning, is a sure -shot strategy. One could use classified/display advertisements, direct mail or printed articles which can be tagged on some of the products. Advertisements in weekly and fortnightly journals in a regular manner can also be effective.

2) **Giving Better Service than the Competitor:** Depending upon the business you have, a good after-sales service gives good business. A satisfied customer is your best advertiser. The reverse is also unfortunately true, thus emphasising the need for maintaining a consistently efficient after-sales service.

3) **Selective Telephoning:** The term refers to advertising yourself to the prospective clients through the telephone with an innovative approach. If it is possible to identify prospective buyers, telephone them and introduce your products. In a number of instances this has proved to be a highly successful strategy. Your persuasive skills will be put to test.

4) **Networking:** This is by far the best way to start a professional service based from your home. Family, friends, relatives, old contacts and office colleagues can all be your promoters. If you have been networking properly, the networking operations can be further strengthened by direct mail, personal letters, thank-you

LAABH HI LAABH

Networking for Best Results

Chand Narain, a reader of 'Laabh hi Laabh', has written to us commending the write-ups and has given his own additional inputs for some. While concluding, he says that 'The truth is that the "Sky is the limit" for whatever one chooses to do'. He could not have been more right. One area where the business can add immense value to their efforts is by resorting to a proper 'networking' whenever they have an opportunity to do so, be it a seminar, a workshop, a business meal, a formal discussion or informal meetings. Business situations always boil down to people situations. A good networking can open many doors to new opportunities which a mediocre networking will miss. Whether it is personal networking or a business networking, a few tips given below will always come handy.

- **Prepare in Advance:** The trick is to be proactive. Anticipate the kind of crowd and interest groups you are likely to meet and think of some areas of mutual interests you can discuss with them. Also determine your objectives for every meetings. Do not head for your comfort zones and go to your familiar crowd. One of your goals should be to meet at least 5 or even more new people during every session.
- **Dress appropriately:** Dress in a manner which will enable you to move around comfortably and make others listen to you with seriousness. Carry your visiting cards and exchange them at appropriate occasions.
- **Smile:** Don't sulk standing lost near the refreshment table but carry a big smile. People should notice your smile first before your suit or tie. Remember, expression matters. Try and obtain maximum 'Smileage' for your business.
- **Converse:** Be friendly, accessible and approachable. A good businessman keeps his guard up while encouraging others to lower theirs. To some, the art of conversation comes naturally while others have to cultivate it. A prior preparation will therefore always come very handy. A good conversationalist does not condemn, criticise or comment adversely. Rather, he always indulges in a bit of praise which does wonders for the sense of hearing of people it is directed at.
- **Listen and Observe:** Learn to listen. Opportunity sometimes knocks very softly. Observe, or as someone has said, listen from your eyes also. Reaching people involves reading people. Observe their body language. Above all, maintain a healthy listen/talk ratio for yourself too.
- **Follow up:** After the networking, follow-up with the people who are likely business prospects. Even otherwise, if someone needs help, be a good samaritan. Remember, when you help others, they also remember.
- **Networking is an Art:** You must try and perfect it and utilise maximum possible time in such meetings to seek potential relationships. The opportunity you might by seeking in the distance might present itself right where you would be standing and talking during the networking sessions.

* By R S Shukla 'The Times of India' 19-04-2001.

notes, newsletters etc. The most important thing in networking is to ensure a regular follow-up even when the prospect of the business is not very high.

5) **Sampling:** It is useful at times to participate in trade shows, exhibitions. Give gifts so that samples of your products are effectively advertised. You can also speak during seminars or meetings or conduct a seminar or news conference to launch your product or service.

6) **Pricing**: Innovative ideas that enable you to offer lower prices can also be useful. This is different from the concept of penetration pricing. At times low prices are offered to get the initial breakthrough. Later, the price can be gradually raised. The subject of pricing is discussed in greater detail later in this chapter.

7) **Using free publicity:** If you have the calibre or the experience to become newsworthy you can utilise the opportunity for obtaining free publicity. These can be achieved through workshops, seminars, interviews, cable T.V., news releases and writing articles.

PRICING YOUR PRODUCT/SERVICE

Key Questions

Those who are familiar with marketing management know that there are 4 Ps. which are essential ingredients for marketing. They are product, price, promotion and place (or distribution). If you have to improve your marketing, you have to ensure that all these four ingredients are improved and you offer a product or service in which a proper balance is struck amongst these four elements.

The most intriguing question relates to the price one should charge on a product/service. People will be giving a plethora of advices to you on how to price your products. Some of these are as follows:

a) Find out what everyone else charges and set your price somewhere in the middle range.

b) Don't set the prices low. If you do that you will have the problem of raising them in future.

c) Charge just above the going rate and assert that you are different.

From the above it will be clear that there are varieties of approaches towards pricing your service or product. You really do not know what to charge. It is like cooking without a recipe. Many sensitive factors have to be balanced until one can reach a figure which suits both the buyer and the customer. It is therefore, necessary to know the different elements to enable you to determine your own ideal personal solution on the price. For this, you will require to spend a fair amount of time and energy. However, you will discover that the right price can be key to your success.

In a market economy, the price of a product or service is mostly determined by the marketplace. However, there is one advantage you enjoy in a home- based business. You can customize your product and you can vary your prices to some extent.

Strategy when a Buyer Complains of Higher Price

If there are complaints that prices are high from a number of customers, you should look into the matter in greater detail and examine your prices to ascertain the genuineness of such statements.

Most of the time, a complaining buyer is not totally aware of the facts. There are many flaws in their perceptions about the prices. It would be advisable to simply ask the buyer questions like, "What price he/she has in mind ? In what way he/she thinks it is too high"? In many cases you will find that the buyer was not aware of a number of points which have a strong bearing on the prices. It may also happen that certain add-ons like packaging or services, which are being offered by you are not necessary. Once you have discussed this subject thoroughly with the customer you will discover that both the sides were ignorant of many facts.

Also, many buyers are not aware of the production process, the time and effort involved and the problems which arise. In most of the cases if a customer is listening with patience, you can explain to him, verifying his doubts. You might even like to use some of the graphs and charts to prove your points. You are therefore, advised not to rush into the matter and reduce the prices straightaway; rather, discuss the matter with the customer and then take the appropriate decision.

PSYCHOLOGICAL FACTORS

You would be surprised by the fact that many of us decide on the prices based on a number of psychological factors and wrong notions rather than on definite concrete inputs. For example, on account of a number of past experiences and parental exhortations during childhood, many of us develop a wrong attitude towards money, which in turn results in our setting low prices.

The fact of the matter is that if you are doing a job and you like doing it, people will happily pay you for your product or service. This is an important factor, which you must repeat to yourself all the time and certainly when you are fixing the prices or revising them substantially.

Do remember that wrong notions get built up from time to time. These are as follows:

1) The work I do can be done by others, so why should I charge too much?
2) How can I make them part with their hard earned money for a simple thing that I am offering?

PRICING PROCESS

In order to determine the prices you must follow a step-by-step procedure:

1) Work out a number of pricing alternatives from the strategies as described earlier.
2) Test each alternative with the respective buyers.

3) Choose the alternative which gets the best response.

4) Continue monitoring till you are satisfied with the results.

5) Check up every quarter your income and expenditure return and the impact of the pricing of the concerned products/services.

A few of the important reasons, which may require you to seriously revise the price either upward or downward are as follows:

a) A buyer commenting " This is a fantastic bargain".

b) Sales are high but profits are low.

c) Demands are high but you cannot meet them (this will require an upward revision).

d) Many customers are complaining about prices.

e) Many customers are complaining about the products/ services, but it may really be on account of price.

f) Many customers lose interest after hearing the price.

Do remember that price is one of the critical features of marketing. If the price is good your business is doing fine. If the price is not working properly your business is not operating properly. Nonetheless you must carry out some basic research. Begin by getting answers to the following questions.

1) What will the customers actually pay?

2) How much is your product or service really worth in concrete terms?.

3) Will you break even with the contemplated price or what indeed is the break even price?

4) Can you alter prices by altering the value? This involves the issue of deciding whether you can do a little for a lot or a lot for a little.

DISTRIBUTION

Place or distribution is yet an important element of the marketing mix. A sound knowledge of market intermediaries and physical distribution is an essential prerequisite for efficiency and cost control. Market intermediaries include wholesalers and retailers in different shapes and forms. Physical distribution involves agencies and practices devoted to transportation and storage. Of late, incoming and outgoing logistics are being increasingly scrutinised by the corporates. An ideal distribution system with appropriate combination of wholesalers and retailers and proper channel management is necessary for business success.

THINGS TO KEEP IN MIND

Your important marketing functions should therefore, cover the following:

1) Develop your marketing plan and strategies you will use for executing the plan. The plan must cover the

four Ps i.e. product (Or service), price, promotion and place (or distribution).

2) Implement a minimum marketing effort every day/ week/month. For example, run a classified advertisement in a local paper each week, call two business clients each day, attend two networking groups per week and send monthly newsletters to your mailing list.

3) Set up a procedure to ascertain how a new client came to know about your business. This will enable you to select the best marketing method.

4) Review your marketing effort every month and reorient.

5) Follow-up, follow-up and follow-up. Whether it is meeting people each week or sending thank-you notes to all, your defined marketing activities must be followed-up regularly without fail. Keep up with your networking and keep your information/database up-to-date.

LAABH HI LAABH

"I Don't Know Who You Are..."

Dr. A.B. Gupta of Gurgaon (details changed at his request), a civil surgeon from Haryana Govt. Health Services retired on December 31, 2000, and settled down at his plot acquired in 1990 and minimally constructed since then. Despite constructing an additional room on the plot after his retirement and starting his clinic in the room, he finds a poor response.

Three things are quite obvious from this letter. Like many other successful people in their long successful early career, Dr. Gupta did not do any post-retirement planning while in service and presumed that he did not need any. If he had done this, he would have possibly discovered that his plot was not located near to his target clientele. Also, he did not promote himself enough with his prospective patients.

This has prompted me to title his response with an extract from the famous book on Marketing Management by Kotler. The quote, in essence, says, "I don't know you, your company, your product, your values, your record or your reputation. Now, what it is it you want to sell me?"

As far as the location of the clinic is concerned, you might like to check if you can shift to a more suitable place closer and conveniently located to your target clientele. If, however, it is not possible or desirable, you may have to resort to a larger marketing effort to promote yourself. To start with make an attractive handbill, describing your essential attributes, achievements, expertise and other details which will be of interest to your patients. Consider the alternative of free advice on certain ailments or to certain section of the people. Circulate it to the prominent people of your vicinity. Use newspaper vendors for putting these bills in the newspapers.

Do this Regularly for a few times

- Make a list of prominent people, opinion-leaders, of your own profession and meet them personally to introduce yourself. Give yourself a target, of say, one or two persons everyday till your practice picks up. Persevere and be patient. Observe proper courtesies such responding on time to calls and letters.
- Join the local medical association and attend meetings regularly and enthusiastically. Follow the tips given in an earlier article on networking to make yourself known and accepted better.
- If there is any special segment of your market which your specialisation can serve better, treat it as your 'niche' market and cultivate it in particular.
- Make a list of prospective industrial, business and government establishments, etc., which might enlist you as a consultant. Contact their chief executives/personnel managers for this. Also, enlist yourself as a visiting consultant with important medical centers which offer such service.
- Attend workshops and seminars on medical matters and contribute effectively. Offer to give lectures on important medical subjects at community centers. Invest some time and energy for contributing some article in local newspapers, magazines and on the cable network of your vicinity. Say something or offer something which is newsworthy.
- The greatest mistake in marketing is thinking that because you can give a good service/advice, people will automatically buy it. If this was so, why would the giant multinationals spend so much on advertisements. Your primary job is to let everyone who needs your service/consultancy know about you and the service in a manner that convinces them to approach you now.

* By R S Shukla 'The Times of India' 12 July 2001.

OOO

chapter 8

finance and accounting functions

Financial Management is also a core function, which can only be neglected at your peril. Get to know the basics and exercise a proper financial control to achieve your business targets.

There is no need to emphasise that if you are in business you must manage your finances very efficiently. A workable record keeping system of your business finances is an absolute must for your business as well as your peace of mind. Also knowledge of elementary financial management is equally important for beginners. If you do not have that, look for a part-time help at least.

To start with, you must separate the business finances from personal finances. In business finances, you must be aware of the flow of your cash, inwards and outwards, in the long, medium or short term. With the personal computers coming in, it is recommended that you computerise your financial management tasks, backed up by paper trails for the auditors as well as income tax authorities.

There are a number of computerised systems available in the market. Select a system which suits your requirements. If you are doing your calculations manually, remember that, if your business grows beyond the point where you are spending more than 30 minutes a day of your time on financial matters alone, you must employ a help or go for computerisation. Finally, the system of financial management adopted by you must be simple and easy, suited to your capabilities, easily expandable and should cover all essential financial information.

AN EASY RECORD-KEEPING SYSTEM FOR FINANCES

A proper record keeping system should:

- Provide all information on finances and cash flow when needed.
- Provide information on banking transactions, bills, invoices, billing made to the buyers, inventory, sales record and long/short-term assets and liabilities.
- Provide paper trails/receipts in available files for income tax authorities and audit etc.
- Provide periodic profit and loss account, preferably one every month and a balance sheet every year.
- Indicate which of your business activities are most profitable.
- Prepare estimated tax returns to enable you to plan the financial requirements. Do try to have adequate knowledge of legally allowed tax deductions to minimise your income tax liabilities.

It will be obvious from the above that unless your financial management system is thorough, easy to manage and gives you information/inputs to plan and run your business you cannot function properly and the business will come to grief sooner or later. No one has succeeded in business unless his financial and marketing management activities have been properly and methodically managed.

BILLING AND FOLLOW-UP

You must be personally committed to a system whereby you can collect the payments for the products or services delivered/ rendered as quickly as possible to enable you to ensure the survival and smooth running of your business. Regular inward cash flow is as important to business as breathing is to life.

However, one may not be able to realise all his bills within the given time. The endeavour should be to collect as much as you can and expedite the outstandings.

The following could also be done to ensure better cash collection:

- Offer discounts for cash payments at the time of delivery or within a specified number of days of delivery.
- Have clear terms for charging higher interest, should a buyer default on payments beyond a specified number of days.
- For every buyer, set a limit on a maximum credit, which could be extended to him and the maximum time that can be allowed to him to settle the dues. If these limits are crossed, stop further supplies/services.
- Check and ensure that bills are raised and sent with minimum delay after the delivery has been made or services rendered. If EDI (Electronic Data Interchange) facilities are available, the same can also be used for preparing bills/ invoices.

GETTING THE MAXIMUM FROM CASH IN HAND

If you are regularly analysing your cash flow vis-a-vis liabilities, you shall know straight away that you have surplus money for investing it in short-term interest deposits. Before transferring this money to a short-term deposit account, check up with other banks in the neighbourhood as well on the interest rate they are offering and make your deposits in the bank that offers the highest interest rate. Keep on reinvesting to make cash on your cash.

Ensure that you have a minimum deposit in the bank at all times, so that the bank fees are avoided. It is advisable not to have an account with banks where ATM charges are levied, since their account maintenance charges are high. Check up with banks, if there are other innovative services being offered by them to increase your returns. With banking services being privatised, many innovative schemes are likely to be offered.

REDUCING YOUR LIABILITIES

It is important to ensure early receipts against your bills since you have to clear your liabilities regularly. Wherever possible, you should also do the following:

- Arrange for interest free or very low-interest credit from the suppliers for the maximum duration as far as possible.
- Ensure that all your idle earning assets are rented or leased to generate cash.

- Ensure timely (but not necessarily immediate) payments of all bills on your firm or yourself. If this is the beginning of the month and the payment is to be made by the end of the month, you should not pay immediately. It would be better to make a post dated cheque immediately but the same could be sent at the later predetermined date.
- Review your stocks from time to time and ensure that they are kept down so that the money is not needlessly locked up in the inventory. Follow an ABC or VED (Vital, Essential, Desirable) concept for inventory management. ABC concept involves a higher degree of control and a smaller inventory of A items, which are costly but less in number. B and C items are those which are comparatively less costly but more in number and hence might not be subjected to that high a control A category items. In a typical inventory of 100 items, 10% items with high cost might be A, 25% B and 65% as 'C' class items.

CATERING FOR CONTINGENCIES

Even if you are the best planner, at times you will find yourself running short of money. To cater for such contingencies you must always have a plan to raise emergency money. This will include raising money through personal loans from banks/ cooperative credit societies, or against assets like NSCs, LIC policies, F.D. receipts, jewellery, units, shares and other securities.

Like-wise, private finances could also be tapped from credit cards, hundies, brokers, visees (illegal but widely prevalent).

CREDIBILITY AND RELATIONSHIP WITH YOUR BANKER

It is absolutely necessary that you have excellent relationship with your banker and maintain a very high credibility with him The money borrowed from the bank must be paid back as per the agreed schedule except in extremely rare case. Even in these cases check if some part-payment can be arranged. It is always advisable to see your bank manager and explain your problems as soon as it becomes evident that you cannot pay the money on the due date.

Need for A Full or Part-Time Accountant

Finally, if you find that your finances are getting complicated or you cannot manage them personally, arrange for a part-time or full-time help. Always insist that you are provided with all essential financial information relating to your business.

OOO

chapter 9

managing relationships in the changed set-up and preventing wrong habits from setting in

Operating from home definitely affects relationships with your nearest and dearest ones. You must therefore anticipate the likely problems and be proactive in resolving them. Similarly, unless you are watchful, you might develop wrong habits and squander away the advantages of working from home. Know the pitfalls and avoid them carefully.

RED ALERT

The change from an office to home routine sometimes results in a person becoming a 'Recluse'. Man is a social animal. It is natural that on shifting to a home-based business, you will miss your formal and informal groups, the chit-chats and the kind of interdependence you had experienced in your previous assignments. It is therefore, absolutely important that a part of your time is spent on such activities, which keep you in contact with other important people and colleagues.

It is also equally important that even while maintaining the twin-hatted routine, you maintain an ideal relationship with your parents, spouse and children. A healthy family relationship can be a very big asset, while the absence of it can be extremely damaging to your mood, morale, health and eventually will affect the business. The changed situation of running the office and home from under the same roof can produce irritants unless managed properly right from the beginning.

In this chapter we shall be discussing the ways and means to ensure that establishment of your home office does not affect your close relationships with your near and dear ones as well as your links with the outside world, which indeed provides a very valuable input to your psychological well-being as well as business success. We shall also be discussing certain other wrong patterns or habits that creep in and the way they can be rectified.

INTERACTING WITH FRIENDS, COLLEAGUES AND IMPORTANT PEOPLE

The above should be achieved by taking concrete action to ensure that you remain in contact with your counterparts in pursuit of useful social or professional activities. This can be achieved by the following means:

- Join associations, social organisations and clubs so that it gives you a chance to improve your personal, technical or commercial knowledge, ensures your regular participation in community activities and maintains your image. It is wrong to assume that these kind of activities are non-productive. Some associations can bring you a huge amount of useful information, general, technical or commercial which can benefit your business substantially.

- You can make it a point of keeping in touch with the people you feel comfortable with. If nothing else, telephone them periodically and exchange information.

- Attend social functions, seminars and workshops. These functions can provide friendship and professional assistance/ inputs and open the way for closer net - working.

If you are in regular touch, you will, at times, be able to get vital tips on your business as well. Information on competitors, products, prices, market situation, industrial relations etc. can be very useful. Besides, a minimum amount of interaction also fills the psychological void and fulfils the basic need of affiliation within you.

THE THINGS YOU MIGHT MISS

It is also necessary to seek and identify what you are really missing when you start working totally from home. Once you have done that, it will be possible for you to take action to replenish these elements partly or fully. Some of the important things you might miss are as follows:

a) Immediate feedback of your good work; a pat on the back.

b) A word of encouragement, an understanding look or formal recognition of good work from your boss.

c) The sense of importance from the status given by big organisations.

d) The sense of belonging to the organisation and the formal/ informal groups you were part of.

e) Testing new ideas and discussions about your performance, thereby improving upon it.

f) Help or moral support in the midst of an emergency.

g) Inside information through the grapevine.

h) Esprit-de-corps or team spirit, the feeling of belonging to a group.

In addition to what has been stated in the earlier paragraphs, you could also try the following:

1) Read useful publications and listen to radio/view T.V. programmes on important features.
2) Use the telephone to talk to people even for soliciting an opinion or reaction. If you are conversant with computer, take an electronic coffee-break talking to people not only in India but abroad as well through the computer.
3) Organise informal meetings at breakfast, lunch, tea or dinner and call your colleagues, friends and other useful people at home. You can also invite these people to visit your home office and, in turn, visit their offices if necessary.
4) Set up a working group to meet on a regular basis.

AVOIDING BAD HABITS, TEMPTATIONS AND EXCESSES

Without realising it, you might acquire certain bad habits while working from home, which will affect your efficiency and output. These habits set in and unless identified and eliminated, become a part of your life-style. It is necessary that you know about them so that you can rectify the situation quickly.

Important bad habits are listed below:

1. Taking too much time in eating the meals.

2. Sleeping late.
3. Taking too many snacks in between the meals, leading to lethargy, and possibly, obesity.
4. Wasting too much time visiting friends, neighbours, talking on telephone or entertaining your own visitors.
5. Putting off important work for the next day or week when it could be performed immediately.
6. Getting addicted to television.
7. Staying in night clothes, giving a sloppy, unshaven and unsmart look.
8. Taking too much time for reading newspapers and magazines.
9. Drinking while working.
10. Working haphazardly instead of planning it for the next day, week or the month with proper prioritising.

As indicated above, quick identification of bad habits setting in is necessary. Ask yourself "Am I eating too much or for too long; or spending too much time with the visitors etc"?

The next step is to take corrective action till you come back to the normal pattern. If you wish to avoid over-indulgence, take the following steps:

a) Work at a relaxed, but reasonable pace.

b) Develop a lifestyle which ensure a positive addiction to healthy and productive habits e.g., walking or jogging, setting a time limit for finishing newspapers, combining a parallel activity while watching television etc.

c) Set up guidelines for taking snacks. Deepak Chopra, internationally famous physician and author of the book *'Perfect Health'* suggests many such guidelines. He advises that you should eat only when you are actually hungry. Sometimes one has the urge to eat snacks, when in fact, he is desiring something else, e.g., taking a break. He proposes that if you are really hungry you should sit down and eat with an intention of enjoyment. You must distinguish between physical hunger and emotional hunger and eat only in case of the former. The best way is to eat exactly what you want to by taking small bits, chewing them thoroughly and enjoying the taste and flavour. You should stop just as you feel slightly full and not to continue till you are overfed.

d) Make sure your entire input during the day i.e. what you eat and drink is within the total calorific requirement and the balanced diet structure of the day providing you with sufficient proteins, carbohydrates, fat, vitamins and minerals.

e) Do something special instead of taking snacks. These include things which are stimulating and give psychological satisfaction. Some examples could be, playing your favorite sport, writing in a diary, seeing a cartoon movie, walking through the neighbourhood, doing something handy in the house, quizzes, antakshari etc.

f) Keep whatever you wish to avoid as far away from your home- office as possible.

g) When giving up a bad habit try and imagine how terrific and different you will feel when you have got rid of it.

MANAGING CHILDREN

Children are an essential part of the family. While it is important that you and your spouse remain busy in work, it is equally important that a part of your time and attention is given to them. It becomes more complicated when you start working from home and have to draw a thin line of distinction between parenthood and career. While it is very satisfying psychologically for the parents as well as children to be in physical proximity at the house, ensure that your work goes on efficiently even if it requires some disciplining, which may temporarily result in friction and resentment.

Noise, interruptions and privacy are the issues, which have to be identified and tactfully dealt with, so that both the sides can adjust to a new set of circumstances. One will have to devise different routines and approaches for young infants, children aged between 6 to 12 years and above 12 years. Some strategies suggested are as follows:

a) Request aged people or adults of the family to help to look after infants and small children.

b) Hire a baby-sitter or a housekeeper. Your child can also be taken to a baby –sitter or a crèche. Alternatively, check if responsible elderly children can come and keep a watch on the youngsters.

c) Trade baby-sitting with a friend or start a child-care co-operative with friends or neighbours.

d) Put the children through a learning process to adjust to your operating from home. They should slowly get rid of the idea that, just because you are at home, you will be available to them totally.

e) There should be no insecurity in the minds of children on account of the new arrangement. You should take steps to remove such elements and insecurity.

Some of the questions, which might trouble children are as follows:

1) Will you (parent working at home) be available when needed by me?

2) Will I still remain important?

3) What are the new 'Do's' & 'Don'ts of the new arrangement?

Obviously handling children is a delicate problem. If they are grown up, discuss the problems arising out of the home office to them and make them a participant in arriving at the new arrangement. You have to be patient in managing the change. It will require weeks or even months. You also have to learn to say 'No' without being harsh or cruel. Above all keep an open mind and remember that making the children unhappy is something which you should avoid totally. If necessary, you may have to shift your office out of the house for the sake of harmony. However, before you do this make sure that you have examined all the other alternatives and moving out has been decided as a last resort.

As emphasised, children should be least affected by the changed routine and even this change must be effected tactfully. Rather than 'office-proofing' your children, you must try and 'children proof' your office. Locate the office at the far end or in the basements. However, when they do venture to drop in, welcome them and convey to them with extreme tact that they are in a more formal place than the home.

ADJUSTING RELATIONSHIP WITH THE WIFE/HUSBAND

One of the most frequent questions a person, who decides to start working from home, is confronted with or should be confronted with is, "How can we make it a pleasant arrangement with the two of us having to see too much of each other everyday?"

It is a fact that even a housewife who has to change her home routine and social schedules resents changes when the husband starts operating from home. The same happens when one or both members of a working couple move over to operate from home. It is obvious that one has to guard against bitterness or tension creeping in on account of changed pattern of work and relationships at home. It is therefore, important to get to a right start just as it is equally important to recognise early warning signs of trouble or when, despite your efforts, things are not improving.

Important Elements of the Change

The important changes that take place as a signal to your deciding to operate from home, would be as follows:

- **Adjusting to new roles:** The man or woman moving in will require a readjustment in the existing relationship and roles. The magnitude of change is most when both partners work at home. It is also seen that when one works at home and the other outside, there are psychological problems coming from, "the grass is always greener on the other side" syndrome.

- **Adjusting to new duties and responsibilities**: This will require sharing of control, duties and responsibilities relating to security, money, children, time, conveyance, space and other domestic resources/duties such as payment of electricity, telephone bills, bank deposits/withdrawals etc.

- **Impact of new Identities:** The changed role of the spouse/ spouses will affect the existing identities and transform them into new ones. Once again, psychologically, this has a major impact on the relationships.

  An appropriate strategy to ensure a smooth change-over should include the following:

- **Make the decision to operate from home a thoroughly participative one**: If you can make the spouse think that it is actually his/her decision, so much the better. It is important that you encourage your spouse to talk about the likely problems, real or imaginary, which are to arise, and discuss the same in detail. One must understand that different people have different perceptions of situations and just because you have been living in the same house does not guarantee that you can appreciate and understand all the aspects of every issue. A number of times the two spouses have different perceptions on a domestic matter. Building trust and an atmosphere of openness is very important. For instance, the wife may not like too much encroachment in the bedroom due to vacation of the place to make your office. You, on the other hand, may be quite convinced that the decision to operate from home is too critical and a seemingly 'minor' issue should not upset it or delay it.

- **Test and evolve the solutions responding to your spouse's concerns**: If necessary, just implement them to see they do. If they don't, modify them and carry out a retest. If they still do not satisfy your spouse's concerns, give them up.

- **Ensure that as you progress and days pass new problems are also tackled in the similar manner.**
- **Ensure total communication is maintained all the time**: This is extremely necessary because your verbal and non-verbal exchanges (e.g. body language) are likely to be 20 to 50 time more per day as compared to the earlier situation i.e., prior to shifting, due to both of you being in the house for a much longer period.
- Ensure that win-win solutions are implemented.
- Make it clear to yourself as well as to your spouse that the problems are temporary and are bound to be resolved.
- Welcome the problems as opportunities and ensure that solutions implemented are clear to all the parties, i.e. you, your spouse and your children.
- Be light-hearted, laugh a lot and retain a sense of humour.

Maintaining Love and Affection

Sometimes due to the preoccupation with your work or business or domestic problems, things start getting sour. You should not allow this to happen and evolve a strategy, which results in continued love and affection with your spouse.

The following steps could be tried in helping to achieve these objectives:

- Respect each other's individuality and take interest in each other's activities.
- Avoid sarcastic remarks. Appreciate the value of silence in place of an angry retort. Kindness will keep the bonds stronger.
- Compliment each other liberally. Don't let a day pass without a few pats on the back.
- Enjoy each other's hobbies. Go for a drive in the evening.
- Have a proper understanding of the business and non-business i.e. totally domestic areas in the house. Likewise, there should also be a proper understanding of the business and non- business times. Don't take business to the bed.
- Have positive feelings. If there are negative sentiments, wait for suitable opportunities to discuss, clarify and resolve them.
- Never let down your spouse in front of others.

WHAT TO DO WHEN THINGS DON'T GET BETTER

At times, in certain cases, it becomes abundantly clear that the relationship is not getting better and is, in fact, turning sour.

One should remember that the basic purpose of working from home is to improve the quality of life of the family in the final analysis and definitely not for making money alone. Some of the early indications are as follows:

- Perception of tension in the domestic environment.
- Bitter exchanges and shifting the blame for the problems to the other partner.
- Break-down in communication and resorting to unimportant work to avoid talking to your spouse.
- Being needlessly formal.
- Pretending to be over busy to avoid sex.
- Talking of extraneous things and not of things which are really on your mind.
- A genuine feeling of jealousy resulting in emotional resentment.

It is necessary that you must nip these problems in the bud. If however, you find that they are not being eliminated, discuss them very frankly with your partner with a positive and fresh outlook. If despite these discussions the problems persist, it would be desirable to seek the help of some elderly experienced person, marriage counsellor or even a psychiatrist. It will be most desirable if both of you see the expert together. However, if your partner has reservations there is nothing wrong in going alone and discussing your problems with the expert. Many times such situations require one of the partners to take the first step.

Finally, if after trying your best it is felt that the office at home is upsetting marital harmony we would recommend you to give up this venture or shift, if you have to, to keep the home intact.

ooo

chapter 10

the final word

Many giant businesses have started from a modest office at home. Besides, for senior retired people or housewives, the practice has given a boost to their quality of life. However, take the step after knowing the physical and psychological problems which might arise. This is one case where prevention is definitely better than cure. Your being prepared enhances your chances of success tremendously.

A home office, comfortable, convenient and functional – along with a customised system can be a great asset for those who wish to operate from home. The concept has already spread in the advanced countries in the West. In our country, due to a variety of reasons, the numbers operating from home is also fast rising. The gradual realisation of its obvious benefits - the saving of time and money. From daily commuting, escape from unhealthy pollution and avoidance of heavy social costs due to long absences from home and family for long hours - is sinking in.

With India on the verge of a huge 'services sector' expansion and also on the threshold of a 'retail revolution' (projection for 2005 – Rs.1,60,000 crores business with more than 80% of the business in unorganised sector expecting a growth of more than 10 million retailers from the existing 5 million), a great opportunity beckons of people to operate from home and strike the gold.

There are however, physical and psychological problems arising due to the location of the 'office' and 'home' both at home. Unless a person understands these problems and is prepared to resolve them effectively, he might find himself bogged down by them and lose efficiency and motivation.

A number of practical suggestions have been made to survey your home and carve out the best office space, if need be, with the help of modifications, partitions, redesigning, relocation or additional constructions. Furnishing and equipping the office will also require creativity and innovation. Do remember that possessing or acquiring entrepreneurial qualities is not enough - one must be able to use them too.

A system is also to be created and implemented to ensure that your home office routine is customised, a graphic identity for you is established and the outsiders visiting you can discern an efficient office atmosphere. This will allay the demotivation arising out of the feeling of the loss of status, besides bringing in the obvious benefits of orderly work with least disturbances from the family, relatives, neighbours and casual visitors.

The biggest challenge comes in managing the change with your spouse, children and immediate relatives staying in the home. The objective should be to arrive at a win-win solution and to obtain a supportive participation from them. A conscious and continuous effort on your part to maintain an ideal atmosphere at home is necessary.

One has to constantly remind himself of the two important evils one can easily fall prey to while working from home. One is of losing contact with the outside world and the other is of developing wrong habits which affect your image and work. The book provides adequate explanations and strategies to overcome these wrong habits. You must adhere to a minimum number of outdoor or field visits to keep the contacts alive and generate more business. At home, make a conscious attempt to identify, at the first instance, any non-productive trend setting in so as to remove it immediately. What is equally important is that, through deliberate efforts, one must keep healthy contacts with a few good social groupings, associations or organisations to be an effective part of the community and also to remain informed on business issues.

Some corporates are realising the immense worth of the contribution the Small Office Home Office (SOHO) can make and are likely to assist in establishing community based recreation centres, clubs, healthcare and support services to help these people from becoming isolationists and losing efficiency. This is a welcome sign. However, till such time these institutions are established, you must identify and associate with your own networking group through your own effort.

If you follow the strategies suggested in this book, you are sure to reap the benefits of saving extra hours and expenses of daily commuting and utilise the same for performing as well on the job as in the formal office or for running a business from home. Appendix 'A' of Chapter 4 gives more than four hundred businesses, you can choose from. Alternatively, there might be production related businesses, which you might like to undertake. The important thing is that you would be running this business from a secure and firm base - your home - and conserving on many resources. Your wife/husband may also chip in, and in the overall sense, there would be more happiness, comfort and earnings.

Last, but not the least, do not forget that as a 'well-informed' and 'well prepared' entrepreneur, you will not only provide employment to a large number of countrymen, but will also be a role model for many other entrepreneurs aspiring for success. Their success will result in generation of wealth, not only for themselves but for the country also. It will also contribute to the concept and movement of the 'Free Enterprise', which is vital for sustenance of democracy in our country.

So good luck, good job, good business and good fun.

LAABH HI LAABH

How to Reduce Costs in Small Businesses

- **Develop and Maintain Vital Information Linkages:** Right from the pre-planning stage, the small business and Industry-owner must plan, develop, update and maintain his vital information linkages relating to the external environment concerning his business. These include his suppliers, customers, competitors, both present and prospective, distributors, transporters, regulatory authorities, financial institutions including banks, legal retainers, service providers, association heads and members, union authorities and politicians.
- **Aim for Maximum Customer Satisfaction:** Always strive to provide maximum customer satisfaction by continuously adding to his perceived benefits. If you can maintain and add to you customer base, you have succeeded in your aim.
- **Maintenance of Quality:** Commitment and attitude of the management towards consistent maintenance of high quality of your product or service is essential. It also reduces the long-term costs. Remember that quality saves, quality sells and quality satisfies. It helps to build your brand image, which in time to come can become your biggest customer-puller.
- **Know Costs:** So many business owners and managers are not aware of the costs of their business operations, inventories, spares, components, raw materials and human and other resources. On the other hand, efficient people are those who have such costs on their fingertips. To cut costs, you must know costs, including those of production holdups, stock-outs and of surplus inventory.
- **Waste Control:** Easier said than done Successful businessmen are those who have the least waste. Recycling or reprocessing the waste can add to your credit side in a big way. If required necessary advise can be sought to cut down the waste.

LAABH HI LAABH

How to Reduce Costs in Small Businesses

- **Ensure Adequate Internal Cash Generation:** There is no use expecting Rs. 2 lakh against your supplier next week when you are critically short of Rs.50,000 today. Ensure a methodical and meticulous follow-up of all outstanding remittances. Organisations tend to neglect proper follow-up of outstanding claims against transportation agencies. In many cases lakhs of claims remain outstanding for years due to inadequate follow-up. All these represent money locked up. The earlier it can be recovered, the quicker it can be reused.
- **Make all your Non-Earning Assets Earn:** You may have idle assets including buildings, machines, manpower and other facilities. Your idle assets can be in terms of surplus inventory, excessive in-process inventory or surplus finished goods. Have proper planning and control of production and materials. The 'Just in Time' concept followed by the Japanese and adopted by a few Indian companies is worthy of emulation. The same, incidentally, is true of money lying idle in your banks. Invest the same in short-terms deposits, if nowhere else.
- **Emergency Money:** Despite all precautions, unforeseen events do occur when you require extra money urgently. Be aware of different sources through which you can realise such money at very short notice. Credit cards, overdraft facilities, personal loans from banks or credit societies, private bodies, lease financing, hundies and pawnbrokers are such sources besides relatives and friends. Remember to clear the loans in their stipulated times or else you might not get them the next time. Maintaining your credibility is a must. If you can't repay, tell the creditor in advance to obtain an extension. Remember that the most valued virtue a creditor expects from a borrower is a consistent reputation of clearing loans in time.
- **Conserve Energy and Water:** You may not have noticed but the consumption and costs of electricity and water keep steadily rising. Keep them strictly under control. Designate one of your subordinates as an 'Energy & Water Conservation Officer', and ask him to give monthly reports.
- **Effective Management of Time:** Cut down your unproductive time to the barest minimum. You lose a considerable time in meetings, telephone calls and attending to visitors. Manage them properly to ensure minimum involvement. Simultaneously, utilise the time available in the first manner. Control your TV viewing, do some other productive work while watching TV, take your business reports/ magazines when traveling or in a waiting room. Above all, use your best time for your most creative work. Early risers in the morning and later sleepers in the nights.

- **Innovate/Add value on all possible Fronts:** Encourage innovative ideas for waste reductions and productivity improvements. Conceptualise your business in terms of primary and supporting activities and see where all value additions can take place. In USA, small business firms save millions of dollars annually due to the close attention given by them on all such improvements. If necessary, hire outside consultants. See if IT or latest technology can be used to add value to your product or service. Examine whether you can affect savings by value analysis or value designing.
- **Examine Strategies and Objectives:** Your ship might be a brilliantly run ship but it is doomed to disaster if it is heading for an iceberg. Examine your strategies and objectives periodically or even at short notice to ensure your long-term strategies and objectives are correct. Where necessary, effect corrections.

* By R S Shukla 'The Times of India' 1 & 8 February 2001.

DISABLED – DO NOT LOSE HOPE

Many small businesses are being successfully managed by marginally infirm, disabled or handicapped persons. In a recent survey in USA, a fair number of people running small businesses from home were found to be suffering from some permanent disability or sickness. Choose an appropriate business which you can run. Do not lose hope.

OOO